To you my fellow servant,

May God bless + use you until He comes.

In Christ,

[signature]

II Cor. 5:20

# Biblical Preaching
## for Today's World

# Biblical Preaching for Today's World

by LLOYD M. PERRY

MOODY PRESS
CHICAGO

# Contents

# Preface

THIS MATERIAL in its original form comprised the Lyman Stewart Memorial Lectures for 1971-72 which I delivered at Talbot Theological Seminary in La Mirada, California. The design of the lecture series formed the boundaries which almost automatically excluded some material, and at the same time made it imperative to include other areas.

For instance, no attempt was made to discuss and evaluate the cybernetic revolution as championed by such men as Marshall McLuhan. The science of communication has developed as a field of study in its own right. It could not be given adequate treatment within the contextual limitations of the material in this series.

The history of preaching has been overlooked by many of our present-day homileticians. Many references to great preachers and periods of great preaching are included in hopes of stimulating the preacher to survey the lives and study the sermons of some of the "preaching giants."

Some of the material in chapters 3 and 4 had been dealt with by the author in earlier publications. This coverage of the subject of sermonic arrangement was foundational for a consideration of the broad area of biblical preaching. It was therefore brought up to date and included within this lectureship.

The eighth chapter attempts to show the relevance of some of the basic concepts of speech correction and oral interpretation to the area of sermonic delivery. These have been generally omitted in previous homiletical works. Previous neglect spoke up for their inclusion here.

Subject matter was added to the original lectures so that the book in its published form would not only challenge experienced preachers but would also serve as a classroom text.

In compiling these lectures, I have drawn from many sources and am indebted to many students, authors, and former professors for their helpful contributions. An attempt has been made to give credit for the material within the limits of memory and research. Omission of such credit has been by accident and not by design.

Biblical preaching has not outgrown its usefulness. The methods may vary, but the message remains the same. God's challenge and call to the preacher still comes through loud and clear, "Preach the Word."

# 1

# Biblical Preaching
# and Its Philosophical Foundations

THE QUALITY, effectiveness, and importance of preaching is being challenged. This is not new, however, for such has been the case for some years. Henry Sloane Coffin said, "There is much current disparagement of preaching, and that among some of the more thoughtful in our churches."[1] The Canadian author, Pierre Berton said, "Sermons today are spiritless, irrelevant, dull and badly delivered."[2] "Someone has remarked that if Protestantism ever dies with a dagger in its back, the dagger will be the Protestant sermon."[3] Helmut Thielicke wrote,

> But it is not only the place where the preaching is done that has been so dubiously relegated to the periphery of life and thus in an organic sense displaced. Actually preaching itself has decayed and disintegrated to the point where it is close to the stage of dying.[4]

In an interview in 1971, James Stewart of Scotland was asked whom he thought to be the great expository preachers in America at this time. His reply to the question was to the effect that in his opinion there were no great expository preachers in America today.

Kyle Haselden expressed somewhat the same sentiments when he wrote, "We have to grant that the general level is still low and that there are today no preachers who have a nationwide reputation and influence comparable to the kind wielded in the past."[5] If this be true, then we are in a sad state.

9

The lecturer making a case for biblical preaching is in the eyes of some like Custer on the plains of Dakota. There is the ever present danger that we will spend so much time with the symptoms of the plight of preaching that we will fail to recognize the real cause of the disease. We must do more than merely bemoan the plight. We must seek to discover some of the real causes behind the disease. It is significant to note that in every period of atrocity and ignorance among the people of God, there is a corresponding lack of really great preaching.[6]

The quality of preaching always declines when the conception of preaching is removed from primary to second stage. The fact is that where the authority of preaching declines, the attempts to make worship liturgical and formal increase. The history of Christianity from the middle of the second century to the Reformation shows that nothing, not even elaborate ritual or ornate buildings, will suffice for the Word of God being preached with power and reality.[7] It may well be as Wallace Fisher has stated, that we have built up a brand of pietism in our churches which resists preaching:

> [It] treats Jesus with respect but avoids personal involvement with him, venerates the Bible but does not study it critically . . . and honors the church as a christening, marrying, and burying society—a 'holy place' filled with memories more sentimental than sacred.[8]

James Stewart takes a far more positive approach to the problem, when he says,

> Do not listen to the foolish talk which suggests that, for this twentieth century, the preaching of Word is an anachronism, and that the pulpit, having served its purpose, must now be displaced by press or radio, discussion group or Brains Trust, and finally vanish from the scene. As long as God sets His image on the soul, and men are restless till they rest in Him, so long will the preacher's task persist and his voice be heard throughout all the clamour of the world.[9]

George W. Truett, speaking at the C. H. Spurgeon Centenary, reminded those assembled for that occasion that Charles Spurgeon felt that there was "no substitute for the Christian pulpit. Not the press with all its triumphs; nor the schools with all their learning; nor the amazing triumphs of science can take the place of Christ's preacher. 'For after that in the wisdom of God the world by wisdom knew not God, it pleased God by the foolishness of preaching to save them that believe.' " He went on to say,

Nor will history let us forget that the halcyon days of Christianity have always been the days of great preachers and faithful preaching. It was so in the days of Tertullian, Chrysostom, Augustine and Ambrose. It was so in the days of Luther, Calvin, Latimer and Jonathan Edwards. It was so in the days of Spurgeon. The dry bones of the valley have ever lived and been clothed with flesh and blood when the right kind of man with the right kind of message has stood in the Christian pulpit. The moral and spiritual safety of a nation and of a word is very largely within the keeping of the Christian pulpit. The Thermopylae of Christianity is the pulpit.[10]

These words summarize the burden which rested upon the shoulders of the preacher's preacher, C. H. Spurgeon. They also summarize the conviction of possibly America's greatest preacher, George W. Truett.

There is a need for powerful, energetic, forceful, biblical preaching.

Biblical preaching emphasizes the content of the message more than its homilectical form or manner of delivery. . . . Biblical preaching utilizes the whole Word of God and basically only the Word. . . . Biblical preaching thankfully uses the findings of devout scholars regarding the origin, transmission, translation, preservation and interpretation of the Sacred Text. . . . Biblical preaching is bound to be doctrinal, because certain great, basic doctrines dominate the Scriptures.[11]

It would appear that the conditions referred to in Amos 8:11 are present with us in this day: "Behold, the days come, saith the Lord God, that I will send a famine in the land, not a famine of bread, not a thirst for water, but of hearing the words of the Lord." In accordance with 2 Timothy 2:15, we need to hear the Word preached conscientiously, continuously, comprehensively, and courageously. "Among the many pressing needs which confront the preacher today, none is greater than the need to proclaim the old, old story in such a way that men will be drawn

to God; to preach it in such a way that they will see its beauty
and power; to preach it in such a way that they will be able to
put its truths into daily practice."[12] It is recognized, however,
that there is no quick road to worthwhile preaching. It is hard
work, but it is wonderfully rewarding. Preaching is at once a
privilege and a punishing responsibility.

### A BIBLICAL BASIS—2 CORINTHIANS 5:1-21

If the preaching is to be powerful, energetic, and forceful, the
following factors should be given consideration. The man who
is to do the preaching should conceive of himself as an ambassador for Christ. Second Corinthians 5:20 reads, "Now then we
are ambassadors for Christ, as though God did beseech you by us:
we pray you in Christ's stead, be ye reconciled to God." An ambassador is a messenger, an interpreter. "Any notion that the
preacher is less than an ambassador of the kingdom of God re-
duces the pulpit from prophetic urgency to timid homilies on
marginal matters."[13] Thus the preacher is a messenger for Jesus
Christ. "We do not go to discuss a situation, but to deliver a
message."[14] He has within his hands a portfolio. We are not dis-
pensers of what some have referred to as Sunday syrup. The portfolio provides the instructions in writing. John Dover put it this
way: "The only equipment we are given as preachers is in the
Bible. It's our job to know it, and there's no excuse for not knowing it."[15]

Like any other ambassador, the preacher is appointed to his
task. Certainly no man is able to herald God's gospel with full
power unless he is under God's call to preach. The kingdom of
God does not rely on self-appointed ambassadors. One of the first
prerequisites of a prophetic preacher is to feel that God has laid
His hand upon him and thrust him out irrevocably into a preaching ministry.

Men do not become preachers merely because they want to
preach. Moses was prepared to do the whole bidding of God—
except to speak. Isaiah beheld the vision of the glory of God but
begged to be excused. Ezekiel pled that he might deliver his message in some other way. Chrysostom shrank from the task for
years. Augustine turned in every direction before he plunged

into preaching. Luther might not have preached at all but for his vow of obedience, and that he was ordered directly to do so. John Knox was pressed into the ministry. Frederick Robertson begged to be excused. I am not saying that if one desires to preach that it follows then that he is not divinely sent. I am only pointing out the fact that most have had a deep personal feeling of being unfit. This humility is part of our security.

It was John Henry Jowett who declared, "I would affirm my own conviction that in all genuine callings to the ministry there is a sense of the divine initiative, a solemn communication of the divine will, a mysterious commission, which leaves a man no alternative, but which sets him in the road of this vocation bearing the ambassage of a servant and instrument of the eternal God."[16]

Ian MacPherson has well said, "The only strings that are pulled in all genuine calls to the preacher's office are the heartstrings. And it is God who pulls them!"[17]

As an ambassador, the preacher has his citizenship in the homeland, not in this earth. This is rather clearly set forth in Phillippians 3:20, "For our conversation [citizenship] is in heaven; from whence also we look for the Saviour, the Lord Jesus Christ." His task as an ambassador is to bring into agreement those who otherwise would be at variance with one another and with God.

A second factor to be considered is the measure of one's ministry of preaching. "If in this life only we have hope in Christ, we are of all men most miserable" (1 Co 15:19). Our view of the future will have a very definite effect upon our present activities and aspirations. The messenger of Christ should measure his ministry in view of eternity (2 Co 5:1-4). He should also measure his ministry in view of the down payment which has been provided for him through the ministry of the Holy Spirit (2 Co 5:5).

An effective preaching ministry should have two clear motives behind it. The first, as set forth in 2 Corinthians 5:10, is fear which stems from the fact of accountability. "For we must all appear before the judgment seat of Christ; that every one may receive the things done in his body, according to what he hath done, whether it be good or bad." The preacher, like others, must give account of his time, his words, and his actions. But beyond accountability, there is also the motivation of acceptability as set forth in 2 Corinthians 5:9 and 11-15. "He died for all, that they which live should not henceforth live unto themselves, but unto him which died for them, and rose again. For the love of Christ constraineth us" (vv. 14-15).

The message of a dynamic preaching ministry should be a message of reconciliation. "And [He] hath given to us the ministry of reconciliation" (2 Co 5:18). What method was employed which made this message possible? "God . . . reconciled us to himself by Jesus Christ" (5:18). What is the meaning of that message? "God was in Christ, reconciling the world unto himself, not imputing their trepasses unto them, and hath committed unto us the word of reconciliation" (5:19). The ultimate purpose behind this message and ministry is "that we might be made the righteousness of God in him" (5:21).

Preaching is that unique procedure by which God, through His chosen messenger, reaches down into the human family and brings persons face to face with Himself. The ambassador for Jesus Christ must present Jesus Christ so that men will know Him, love Him, trust Him, and yield their lives to Him in obedience to His Word.

Our business is to preach Christ. He is to be the burden of our ministry. MacPherson has charged us to preach Christ evangelically, as Saviour and Lord; to preach Christ ethically, as Teacher and Example; and to preach Christ eschatologically, as destined Judge and Ruler of the world.[18]

## DEFINITIONS

It will be profitable at this point for us to clarify our meaning of preaching, homiletics, and the sermon. Several definitions have been presented by homiletic writers. T. Harwood Pattison wrote, "Preaching is the spoken communication of divine truth with a view to persuasion."[19] Henry Ward Beecher contrasts teaching and preaching by stating that teaching imparts knowledge while preaching seeks to go beyond that and to change lives. The late Andrew W. Blackwood stated that preaching is divine truth voiced by a chosen personality to meet human needs. Phillips

Brooks, in his classic Yale lectures on preaching, stated that preaching is the communication of truth by man to men. In his presentation, Brooks highlighted two elements involved in preaching: namely, truth and personality. When we undertake to preach a sermon, we set ourselves to the task of convincing the judgment, kindling the imagination, moving the feelings, and of giving powerful impulse to the will, in order that the listeners will be stirred to give expression to their feelings in finer forms of action.

It was Matthew Simpson, in his lectures on preaching, who stated that preaching is not merely the delivering of a message, but it is the delivery of a message by a man who professes to have felt its power and testifies to its truth in his own experience. Preaching to people is an expression of concern for them and of love for them. Love going out finds love in return.

An examination of Ephesians 4:11 and 1 Corinthians 12 will highlight some conclusions regarding the total task of the Christian minister:

> As an APOSTLE *he is to challenge the will;*
> as a PROPHET *he is to probe the conscience;*
> as an EVANGELIST *he is to woo the heart;*
> as a PASTOR *he is to care for the soul;*
> as a TEACHER *he is to inform the mind.*[20]

The total task of the ministry demands the dedication of the total man. Preaching is not a minor matter. It is a matter of major proportions.

Theoretical homiletics speaks of preaching as a science based upon the fundamental principles in the application of rhetoric to homiletics. Sermons are more than speeches, but they are not less. Practical homiletics in contrast with theoretical homiletics speaks of preaching as an art. Homiletics has been defined as rhetoric applied to sacred discourse.

There are differences between great preaching and great oratory. Possibly one of the greatest is that the preacher, having a clear view of his purpose, proceeds to sink himself utterly out of sight behind that purpose. Oratory has a tendency to draw attention to itself. This may be one reason for Thornton Wilder to declare that rhetoric has ruined religion. The principles of homiletics have been gleaned through analysis of the best sermons in every age of the church. Homiletics is the science which treats the nature, classification, analysis, construction, and composition of the sermon.[21] It is the science of which preaching is the art, of which the sermon is the product.

A sermon is a systematic oral address, adapted to the popular mind and based on biblical truth.[22] There are propaganda sermons by which the minister sets out to put something over on the congregation. There are pugnacious sermons through which the preachers wage campaigns, attack enemies, and assail the citadels of those who disagree. These are warlike in nature and vehement in presentation. We need, however, more sermons that deal with people's problems, meet their difficulties, answer their questions, and help to heal their hurts. These will be the sermons adapted to human needs and applying the principles of the Word of God to daily experience. They are prepared and presented for the purpose of persuading men to believe and to act upon the truth that is revealed.

The sermon is the explanation, illustration, and application of God's Word. The sermon that has been formulated with care will have unity, coherence, and proportion. It is scriptural, constructive, persuasive, direct, and personal.

Six rhetorical processes are combined in the formulation of a sermon: narration, interpretation, illustration, application, argumentation, and exhortation.

Preaching is divine truth unfolded by the Holy Spirit through a God-chosen personality to meet human needs. For instance, the preacher's business is not only to discuss repentance, but also to persuade people to repent. The preacher's task is to help the Spirit of God bring to pass in the lives of the listeners that which is the concern of the sermon. A lecture is concerned with a subject to be elucidated, but a sermon is concerned with an object to be achieved.

The ideal sermon involves animated conversation with an audience concerning some vital problem of life where the Word of God sheds light. This type of biblical preaching demands a clear apprehension of the original, historical meaning of the text or passage being expounded. It demands an awareness of the theological depth of the text or passage. It demands that the passage must have its message communicated to men of the present day. The biblical sermon goes beyond the bare historical meaning of the text and interprets it in terms of the contemporary situation. Only the preacher is still operating under the mistaken idea that folk come to church desperately desirous of discovering what happened to the Jebusites. We as preachers should relate both to the Bible and to the contemporary world.

How can we classify sermons? We agree with James M. Hoppin, when he says, "In no part of the science of homiletics is there more of confusion than in the attempt of authors to classify sermons according to their intrinsic qualities—their essential form and treatment."[23]

If we were even to try to name some of the types of sermons heard on occasion, let alone trying to classify them, our task would be difficult. There might be the *butterfly sermon* in which the preacher flits from book to book not lighting too long at any spot lest someone should catch him. There is what Jeff D. Ray called the *Old Mother Hubbard sermon*. In this, the preacher uses each word as a jumping-off place into extended elaborations of disjointed items. There is the *bag of beads message* which consists of a number of good ideas without a string to tie them together. There is the *persecution sermon structure* in which the preacher stays with a verse until persecuted and then flees to the next. There is also the *majoring on the minutia method*. This emphasizes the items picked up by an exegetical microscope so that as Thomas Hobbes once said, "the preacher casts atoms of Scripture as dust before men's eyes, thereby making everything more obscure than it is."

The type of sermon used up to the third century was termed a homily. This was free and informal in organization and delivery, but it was not unstudied. It was usually a running commentary. This could be either a verse-by-verse or a subject commentary. In more recent years sermons have been classified from the standpoint of the manner of handling the text into topical, textual, inferential, and expository.

The topical sermon originated as a method of preaching about

A.D. 1200. In this type of sermon the theme is drawn from the text, but it is discussed independently. It embraces a single leading idea which can be expressed in a verse, proposition, or sentence. It has been regarded through the years as the most oratorical species of pulpit address. Blackwood said that the greatest preachers of all time have been topical preachers. It may well be true that in the history of preaching, topical sermons have outnumbered all the rest. It has been, for instance, almost universally the method of the French pulpit. One of the outstanding dangers in this type of sermon, of course, is that of inventiveness at the expense of scriptural authority. The books, *A Treatise on Homiletics,* by Kidder, and *The Preparation of Sermons,* written by Blackwood, give a good comprehensive coverage of this type of sermon. The late Harry Emerson Fosdick was possibly one of the best masters of the topical method in modern times. While topical preaching can be kept on the high level, it often descends to the level of the periferal and sometimes even the sensational.

The textual sermon follows closely the language of the text, clause by clause, and word by word. Its chief divisions are based upon principle words or clauses within the text itself. It honors the Word of God by keeping near to it and dwelling upon it. It is especially applicable to texts concerning precepts, commands, promises, and warnings. Sometimes it becomes a refuge for ministerial idleness, and can tend toward narrowness and shallowness of teatment.

*Homiletics and Pastoral Theology* written by Shedd, and *Preaching Angles,* by Caldwell, present a fair coverage of the textual sermon. Caldwell suggests, among other things, that the length of the passage being treated is the main distinction between the textual and the expository sermon.

The inferential sermon is one in which the text is the subject, and the discussion consists of the series of inferences drawn directly from the text. The sense of the text must be clearly and plainly fixed before any inferences are drawn from it. The inferences must be in accord with the true sense of the text and the broader testimony of scripture.

The expository sermon aims at making a passage of scripture cling to the listener's mind and heart. It not only makes ancient truth clear, but brings that truth into the present. It encourages the preacher to study large portions of the Word of God, both analytically and synthetically. Such a sermon should present the results of exegesis and not the process. Three books which give a rather comprehensive discussion of this type of sermon are *A Treatise on Homiletics, Homiletics and Pastoral Theology* (both previously cited), and *A Treatise on the Preparation and Delivery of Sermons,* by Broadus, written in 1889.

There has been considerable discussion and controversy through the years regarding the correct definition of an expository sermon. Dr. Charles Koller, who taught homiletics at Northern Baptist Seminary for fifteen years, states that the only preaching worthy of the Christian pulpit is expository preaching. As mentioned earlier, Blackwood said that the greatest preachers of all time have been topical preachers. The young preacher then faces a dilemma. Will he strive to be a worthy preacher or a great preacher? Actually these men both favored biblical preaching. Koller's emphasis was that the passage on which the sermon was to be based should have an organic and thematic unity. Dr. Blackwood recognized that the great preachers developed a theme in their sermons. Having searched for a single definition of an expository sermon, I have now come to the conclusion that there are almost as many different definitions as there are books written on the subject. The definition of an expository sermon depends upon the particular book to which you are referring at the moment.

## An Historical Survey of Expository Preachers

A survey of the preaching of some of the great expository preachers will provide some idea of the nature of an expository sermon from the point of view of the history of preaching.

Origen (184-254) has been regarded as the "Father of Expository Preaching." It has been said that he gave form to the sermon. Athanasius (297-373) employed Origen's concept of expository preaching. Augustine (354-430) possessed real expository skill. His preaching was always close to the people. Directness and conversational tone were characteristics of his style.

Chrysostom (347-407), whose real name was John of Antioch, was essentially an expository preacher. Sixty-six of his homilies remain. In his exposition he moved away from the allegorical approach and toward the critical. Zwingli (1481-1531) was a powerful expository preacher. His preaching was noted, among other things, for its simplicity of language. John Calvin (1509-64) was a biblical preacher noted for sound doctrine. It has been said that he presented the ablest, soundest, clearest expositions in a thousand years of preaching. Thomas Adams (1580-1664) was a biblical expositor as were Thomas Goodwin (1600-80), and Matthew Henry (1662-1714). John Howe (1630-1705) was a good biblical preacher and one of the most brilliant expository preachers of all time. He wrote out his introductions and conclusions in full and the body of the sermon in brief. He worked sixty hours on the preparation of each sermon. He preached fifty-two years in one church. Charles R. Brown (1855-1947) employed the expository method. B. H. Carroll (1843-1914) was one of the greatest biblical preachers of all time. He was original, comprehensive, and thorough in his discussion of his themes. John Cotton (1584-1652) was scholarly and expository in sermon preparation. He is regarded as having been one of the most distinguished preachers of his day. Harry A. Ironside (1876-1951) was known for his expository preaching. His method of preaching was to explain, then illustrate, and finally apply. F. B. Meyer (1847-1929) was an expository preacher known for his evangelistic emphasis. A. T. Pierson (1837-1911) was a Bible expositor with a great missionary interest and emphasis. Gipsy (Rodney) Smith (1860-1947) became a master of simple, persuasive English and is remembered for his expository preaching as well as for his evangelism.

## CHARACTERISTICS OF EFFECTIVE BIBLICAL PREACHING

Our main concern should be that the sermon is biblical, logical, and practical. The label by which it is identified is not the important feature! Paul Rees, writing for *Christianity Today*, stated five key elements of the effective sermon. The first is *relevance*. (He rightly warns, however, that the church which is married to the spirit of one age will find herself a widow in the next.) The second element is that of *concreteness*. This can be developed by being very exact in our choice and use of words. The third element is *vivid word pictures*. The fourth is that of *texture,* by which he refers to the "feel" of the sermon. The fifth and final element is that of *lucidity*. As the sermonizer gives way to the lure of lucidity, he will make certain that his sermons go toward a goal. He will strive to be simple, cultivate the concrete, plan for progression, and emphasize application.[24]

I would like to suggest that effective biblical preaching must be characterized by being *personal*. MacPherson has well said, "To us as sermon-artists our hearers are both canvas and patrons, at once the materials on which our paintings are executed, and the public who inspect and appraise them. Hence for a double reason the people deserve our close concern."[25]

M. Reu wrote that "Preaching is fundamentally a part of the care of souls, and the care of souls involves a thorough understanding of the congregation. The preacher . . . must be a faithful pastor."[26] That which comes from the heart is most likely to go to the heart. Power in the pulpit comes partly through the preacher being able to speak from experience. Sanford gives the essentials for a preacher as being:

1. The preacher's own sure knowledge of personal salvation and holy calling in his own life.
2. A truly deep devotional life for himself.
3. A constant contact with men in their work-a-day-world.
4. The spirit of self-giving and self-sacrifice.[27]

The preacher cannot change lives by eloquent hearsay. He cannot share what he does not possess or reveal what he has not seen.

It is imperative that the preacher know his prospect as well as his product. When the preacher doesn't realize the necessity for knowing the ones to whom he is presenting his message, much that he proclaims just doesn't matter. In many cases it might just as well not be said. This has prompted some to refer to the pettiness of the pulpit.

The preacher should study his audience and with the help of the Spirit of God adjust his presentation, depending on whether they constitute a believing, apathetic, doubtful, or hostile group. This involves the sermonic process of application which is the relating of the eternal truth, discovered by investigation and elucidated by interpretation, to the environment of the congregation in front of the preacher.

Effective biblical preaching must be *purposeful.* One's philosophy, aim, or goal will govern the material that he will use and the method that he will employ. The rule is to begin with one's purpose and not with one's plan. Morgan quotes Rousseau's recipe for a love letter as a recipe to be avoided in sermonizing. The recipe reads: "You will begin without knowing what you are going to say and end without knowing what you have said." A sermon characterized by purposefulness will be unique in its message, unique in its spirit, and will aim at godly living.

Effective biblical preaching should be *persuasive.* The word *persuasive* comes from two root words, meaning "by sweetness." There are several ways of getting people to do that which we want them to do. This may be done through force, through physical structuring of the situation, through forced imitation, through simple expression, through oral persuasion, or through personal involvement.

But possibly the seventh and most important and powerful means is through love. Love is the more excellent way. Henry Drummond (1851-97) referred to it as "the greatest thing in the world." The hymn of love (1 Corinthians 13) emphasizes the fact that love makes our actions profitable for time and eternity. Eloquence, prophecy, and even martyrdom produce nothing of value without love. Love sanctifies every gift. Love marks our characters as being Christian. Love provides an assurance of victory. Faith minus hope and love is intellectual conviction. Hope minus faith and love results in a dream. Love minus faith and hope is passion. All three: faith, hope, and especially love are needed.

Effective biblical preaching must be *prophetic.* The decline in preaching power is due to the ignoring of the Holy Spirit as the supreme inspirer in preaching. A good preacher does not simply use the Spirit, he is used by the Spirit. Corwin Roach asked the question, 'How much dynamite is there in our preaching, blasting away the evil, preparing the way for the good? So often all that we have is the fuse. We lack the proper charge. We are dud shells or blank cartridges."[28]

The analogies referring to the Holy Spirit have meant a lot to me through the years. In John 3 He is likened to the wind which stirs. In Acts 2 He is likened to fire which purifies. In Isaiah 61 He is likened to oil which invigorates. In Revelation 22 He is likened to water which refreshes. We need stirring, purifying, invigorating, and refreshing in our preaching.

The Spirit-filled church described in Acts 2:1-47 provides a profitable context or setting for powerful preaching. The ministry of that church was marked by enthusiasm and a missionary emphasis (Ac 2:1-13). The message (Ac 2:14-37) was prayer supported, Bible-centered, and emphasized the victorious resurrection of Christ. It is no wonder that such a message resulted in conviction. The membership of that Spirit-filled church (Ac 2:38-47) could be identified by their qualifications (v. 38), their activities (v. 42), and their attitudes (vv. 44-47). If a few people were really to get on fire with the gospel, no board of underwriters could measure or estimate the results of such a conflagration.

I stood in the evening darkness at the foot of Glacier Point in Yosemite National Park. The lights had been turned out, and we waited in the darkness for the avalanche of burning coals to fall from the high point down the valley. A voice cried out in the night, "Let the fire fall." Another voice came back through the darkness, "The fire falls." I watched that avalanche of burning embers being pushed over the edge of the point to fall like a great wall of fire. I will never forget that amazing sight as we saw the fire fall. I say today as I did that night, "Let God's fire fall."

## Reading List

Abbey, Merrill R. *Living Doctrines in a Vital Pulpit.* Nashville: Abingdon, 1965.

Allen, Arthur. *The Art of Preaching.* New York: Philosophical Library, 1943.

Berton, Pierre. *The Comfortable Pew.* Philadelphia: Lippincott, 1965.

Blackwood, Andrew W. *The Fine Art of Preaching.* New York: Macmillan, 1937.

————. *The Preparation of Sermons.* Nashville: Abingdon-Cokesbury, 1946.

Broadus, John A. *A Treatise on the Preparation and Delivery of Sermons.* New York: Harper, 1944.

Caldwell, Frank. *Preaching Angles.* Nashville: Abingdon, 1954.

Coffin, Henry S. *Communion through Preaching.* New York: Scribner, 1952.

Fisher, Wallace E. *Preaching and Parish Renewal.* Nashville: Abingdon, 1966.

Haselden, Kyle. *The Urgency of Preaching.* New York: Harper & Row, 1963.

Hoppin, James M. *Homiletics.* New York: Don Mean, 1881.

Jowett, John H. *The Preacher: His Life and Work.* New York: Harper, 1912.

Kidder, Daniel P. *A Treatise on Homiletics.* New York: Carlton & Lanahan, 1866.

Malcolmson, William L. *The Preaching Event.* Philadelphia: Westminster, 1968.

Miller, Donald G. *The Way to Biblical Preaching.* Nashville: Abingdon, 1957.

Morgan, G. Campbell. *Preaching.* New York: Revell, 1937.

Shedd, William G. T. *Homiletics and Pastoral Theology.* New York: Scribner, Armstrong, 1873.

Stewart, James S. *Heralds of God.* London: Hodder & Stoughton, 1946.

Thielicke, Helmut. *The Trouble with the Church.* Trans. and ed. by John W. Doberstein. New York: Harper & Row, 1965.

# 2

## Biblical Preaching
## and Its Biblical Orientation

IT IS UNFORTUNATE that we have not made more of an attempt to
correlate the best of classical rhetoric with homiletical theory.
There has been a trend developing in homiletical writings. This
trend has evidenced a departure from the classical sources. This
can be illustrated in the revisions of the traditional textbook on
preaching by John A. Broadus, *On the Preparation and Delivery
of Sermons.* Each reviser of that text has deleted an additional
number of references to the classics. This took place both with
Dargan's and John Weatherspoon's revisions. A thesis written at
Michigan University by Raymond McLaughlin traces these
changes.

A survey has been made of sixty-eight text and tradebooks in
homiletics written in America between 1834, when Ebenezer
Porter wrote the first American textbook in homiletics, and 1954.
The references to the classical rhetoricians were tabulated, and it
was found that Cicero's works were most often referred to. We
have normally said that the rhetoric of Aristotle formed the most
popular base for modern public address theory. This survey
showed 205 references to Cicero and only 103 to Aristotle. There
were 119 to Augustine and 101 to Quintillian's rhetorical contributions. Whately, Fenelon, Campbell, and Plato had references
to their rhetorical works in that numerical sequence. Homileticians of the past did refer to the classics as these statistics show.[1]

Classical rhetoric involves a study of the theory of speech making. It divides this theory into five divisions. These are implicit
in Greek rhetoric and explicit in Roman rhetoric. The first of

these divisions is *invention*. This deals with the discovery of various means of persuasion and with the gathering of material to be used in the development of the speech. This is the concern of this second chapter. The second part of oratory is *arrangement*. This deals with the organization of material discovered into logical and topical progression. It is my feeling that the writers in homiletics have not dwelt upon this aspect of sermonizing in a sufficient manner. Recent books on homiletics have emphasized the philosophy of preaching more than the methodology of sermonizing (Chapter 3). *Style* is the third part. This is the process of phrasing, in language, the ideas invented and arranged. A rather comprehensive article on sermonic style in contemporary terms is included in *Baker's Dictionary of Practical Theology*.[2] The fourth division of rhetoric is *memory*. This deals with the retention of ideas or thoughts in such a way that they can be reproduced. Preaching without notes would be one way in which this rhetorical emphasis is evidenced in preaching as set forth in the works by Richard Storrs, Clarence McCartney, and Charles Koller. The fifth and final division is *delivery*. This involves the presentation of the ideas which have been invented, arranged, phrased, and memorized. It is concerned with both the audible code of speech (phonetics) and the visible code of speech (gestures). The final chapter in this book will deal with some of the aspects of this fifth division of rhetoric.

This particular chapter deals with the concept of invention. Some of the items of homiletical theory which might be considered under such a heading include sources and kinds of texts, subjects, themes, the classification of sermons, the functional elements of the sermon, methods of preparation, and how to search the scriptures homiletically.

## GENERAL PREPARATION

The origination or discovery of a sermon idea involves both general and specific preparation on the part of the preacher. General preparation involves a general cultural development, whereas specific preparation involves a mental mastery of the specifics to be used in the particular planned address.

Some of the general sources to which the preacher may go for material include observation, reading, and cultural involvement. He will want to read in the classics, biography, philosophy, history, poetry, and fiction. There will be a need for his establishing a firm grounding in all aspects of theology. He will want to study contemporary life by observing trends and individuals. In his book *Preaching Unashamed,* Joseph Sizoo said that a preacher must know at least four things, namely, his times, his Bible, his gospel, and himself. Newspapers and periodicals will be of assistance; also he should read great printed sermons and the printed orations of effective speakers. One of the ways of learning to preach and gain preaching material is by surveying and studying the preaching of others.

Gerald Ray Jordan in his book *You Can Preach* says that one of the main reasons for failures in the pulpit is that many preachers do not diligently study the history of preaching. Several in the field of secular public address as well as in the field of pulpit address have likewise advocated learning to preach by reading the sermons of others and listening to them preach. Andrew Blackwood said,

> Ideally every minister ought to know something about homiletics and more about the art of preaching, but he should think most of all about the sermon. He ought to look on himself not as a scientist with a mass of knowledge, or an artist with a gift of appreciation, but as a preacher with an ability to prepare all sorts of sermons. In order to do such work again and again, he ought to study the sermons of other men and then form habits all his own.[3]

In *Sermons Preached Without Notes,* Koller said, "This volume of sermons has a two-fold purpose. First, there is the obvious purpose of communicating Biblical Truth to bless the lives of the readers. Beyond this, it is hoped that ministers of the Gospel will find these sermons helpful from a structural point of view and for illustrative material."[4]

James Hoppin in *The Office and Work of the Christian Ministry* said that the preacher, especially the young preacher, should strive to comprehend and combine the excellencies of the different kinds of preaching of all times and ages, and to enrich and elevate his own preaching by imitating what is good in them.

Robert Dabney encouraged his students to read sermons written by Samuel Davies, John Mason, and Robert South since he felt that these men were masters of sermonizing. Henry Graves felt that his students should read the sermons of Beecher, Brooks, Spurgeon, and Maclaren for the same reason.

Arthur Hoyt, in his book *The Work of Preaching,* recommended that the preacher would find it profitable to select one or two men such as G. H. Morrison who in some way spoke to him with special profit. He should make these preachers his companions by reading all that he could about them and what they had written. He would thus be encouraged to think their thoughts, speak their language, and receive the impression of their personalities. Hoyt felt that these selected homiletical companions would become for the preacher a source of profitable guidance toward the improvement of his own presentation.

Among the classical writers in the field of rhetoric, Augustine, in his book *De Doctrina Christiana,* set forth his conviction that public speaking is best learned by studying Christian speakers. Good style in preaching is more caught than taught, and this by exposure to the great speakers. This work by Augustine was the last significant homiletical work for a period of 700 years following its date.

Witherspoon in his *Lectures on Moral Philosophy and Rhetoric,* stated that he felt that the best form of training is a wise study and imitation of great models. This same advice and enthusiasm was shared by Edward Tyrell Channing, who occupied the famous Boylston Chair of Rhetoric at Harvard University.

There are several reasons for the study of the sermons preached by others. One of these involves the development and enrichment of the preacher's own devotional life. Another is the opportunity to see how others have successfully communicated the gospel. A study of the sermons preached by others will provide guidance in formulating homiletical patterns or structures. The sermonizer will also glean helpful insights in biblical interpretation both from the standpoint of subject matter and methodology.

The open secret of the success of many preachers is that they put their strength and time into collecting suitable materials for discourse. From the beginning of his ministry, the preacher should have morning study hours. No less than four hours a day for five days a week should be set aside for personal, spiritual upbuilding through prayer, study, and Bible reading. The preacher must first be a listener to God.

One famous preacher gained poise and power in the pulpit by spending an hour in preparation for every hundred words that he wrote in his sermon. Haste is one of the real vices of our time. We seem to be afraid to spend time in quiet reflection. We must think with our watches in our hands. Great sermons are not written in busy streets.

Homiletics books have offered the following additional suggestions for enhancing one's preparation for preaching:

1. Think while walking.
2. Keep notebooks for ideas. (One of these notebooks may be for illustrations and another may be likened to a homiletical nursery bed where sermon seeds can be planted.)
3. Systemize one's use of time.
4. Spread the preparation of a sermon over days rather than hours.
5. Make use of the biblical languages.
6. Mark the books you read in order that you may locate the material at a later time.
7. Give thoughtful consideration to the acquisition of books.
8. Pay attention to the needs of the people.
9. Sermonize when the mind is clear.
10. Take notes while reading.
11. Emphasize the study of truth rather than error.

The sermonizer first gathers the materials of which the sermon is to be composed and then selects what is most fitting. He then arranges the material in a logical order.

### SPECIFIC PREPARATION

The process of specific sermon preparation involves the crystallization of a sermon starter. This is an area, need, or idea which is laid upon the mind of the sermonizer as being a possible foundation for a specific sermon. This sermon idea may come directly from a passage of Scripture, from a series of passages containing a basic unity, or from a source located outside the confines of Scripture. If the sermon starter comes from a source outside the Bible, the sermonizer will then go to the Scriptures and determine the location and the extent of coverage given to this idea within the context of the Scripture itself. He must bear in mind at all times the fact that his task is not to give good advice but rather to present the good news.

Effective sermonizing demands that the preacher develop a homiletical mind. Such a mind will make him aware of sermonic ideas as he reads and observes. It will also assist him in making all resources, both general as well as specific, contributory to the work of sermonizing.

The sermonizer should seek the Holy Spirit's guidance to a passage of Scripture. This passage will not only serve as the basis for his sermon but also as the Scripture lesson to be read in the worship service. He will often begin his study with a long passage and then shorten the passage as his study directs. Longer passages are more useful for expository purposes. The Bible is a large book consisting of 66 books, 1189 chapters, 31,176 verses, and containing 2,930 different characters. In order to cover the Scriptures so that the congregation will appreciate the contents of the entire book rather than merely one section, the biblical preacher should work on large segments of Scripture. His points for his message may come from just one verse, but the surrounding verses should be used to provide helpful biblical orientation.

The amount of Bible content within a sermon should be a matter of real concern. I fear that many congregations are overfed and undernourished. They have heard many sermons but the Scriptures which provide the vitamins for the soul have been omitted. Langdon Gilkey says,

> All around us we see the church well acclimated to culture: successful, respected, wealthy, full, and growing. But are the transcendent and the holy there? In the area of belief we find widespread indifference to the Bible and ignorance of its contents— and strong resentment if a biblical word of judgment is brought to bear on the life of the congregation. . . . Sadly enough the evidence supports the cynic who said that the church in American

society is the easiest club to enter and the hardest from which to be expelled.[5]

The Lord Jesus made the needed emphasis very clear. As Satan proceeded to test Him, the Master gave a ringing reply three times in those first eleven verses of Matthew 4 "It is written," "It is written," "It is written." We must never underestimate the power and authority of the Word of God. Christ knew the Word, He believed the Word, and He obeyed the Word. Satan took his flight.

What constitutes a good preaching portion? It must be a passage which has logical unity. Each paragraph has one main idea. Therefore a preaching passage should consist of one or more complete paragraphs. The boundaries of a preaching portion can often be determined by noting sudden shifts of style. Some passages of Scripture seem to have more homiletical possibilities than others. The following list of identification marks of a preaching portion is suggestive but certainly not exhaustive: (1) *a direct or indirect reference* to a personal, community, or national problem which needs a solution; (2) *a spiritually significant word* which, when clarified as to meaning, will provide help for the listener; (3) *a principle or precept* which needs amplification, illustration, or application.

## SURVEY OF THE CONTEXT

It is wise for the preacher to bear in mind the fact that truth content is not in itself indicative of profitable preaching possibilities. It must be truth which has some practical meaning to the preacher and application. There are three stages in sermonic construction: investigation involves the "then," interpretation involves the "always," and application involves the "now." If the preacher has determined the preaching portion from which he is to construct his sermon, his next task is to study that preaching portion. This involves, first of all, a survey of the context. There are three steps involved in this process of surveying the context of the passage of Scripture. The homiletician will find the book by Don Wagner entitled *The Expository Method of G. Campbell Morgan* helpful reading at this point.

The first step is *to survey the group of Bible books* in which the particular book is located. For example, when preparing to preach on a passage in the book of Ephesians, he should get a general grasp of the dates, emphases, and features of the four prison epistles of which Ephesians is one. A good book of Bible introduction will help provide information for the preacher at this point. Two books, *New Testament Survey* by Merrill Tenney and *Bible Survey Outlines* by Roland Hudson, will prove helpful.

The second step is *to survey the particular Bible book* in which the preaching portion is located. Answering the following questions will prove profitable.

1. What is the main theme of the Bible book? Read and reread it until the main teaching can be crystallized in your thinking, and then summarize it in a sentence.
2. What can you learn about the writer of the Bible book?
3. To whom was the book originally sent?
4. Are there any particular or important repeated terms in the text?
5. What does this book teach about God?
6. What is the nature of the general content of the book? Is it argumentation, exhortation or instruction?
7. Are there evidences within the book of manners and customs of those to whom it was written?

It is helpful to formulate a broad, general outline of the book, giving special attention to changes of subject matter, personages, and places which may help in the determination of the outline. Then several outlines which others have formulated can be compared in order to discover similarities in outline divisions.

The third step is *to survey the context of the preaching portion.* Koller in his book, *Expository Preaching Without Notes,* has listed seven items which he terms factual data. The sermonizer should check each of these seven items. When he has discovered the material, he will then want to collect it and keep it in written form, both for use in the immediate sermon and for future reference. The items of factual data represent the absolute minimum of work one must collect in preparing a passage for preaching. He should first determine the *speaker or writer* of the passage. The type of person represented by the writer may give a valuable clue to the major thrust of the passage and its possible application. He should then determine *the ones* to whom the passage was first *addressed*. The type of person or group who first received the message may be discovered in the congregation to which the preacher is scheduled to present this particular sermon. Establish an *approximate time* for the incident or for the presentation of the original message. The homiletician will want to list other significant biblical and extrabiblical events which took place just before and just after this particular occasion. He will want to locate the place *where the incident took place* or where the passage was presented. It would be helpful to list other significant events which took place at the same or nearby locations. Then clarify the *occasion* which prompted the contents of this passage. Similar conditions may exist in connection with the ones to receive the sermon based upon the passage. He will then want to determine the *aim or purpose* behind the passage. Was the purpose accomplished? Is that same aim or purpose relevant to the lives of the listeners today? Then formulate the *main theme* (subject) of the passage. This will be a phrase which summarizes its content.[6]

There are two additional items which also may be checked. He may want to discover any recent archeological findings which might have bearing upon the interpretation of the passage. And finally, he will want to note any distinctive doctrines, ideas, and stylistic traits of the biblical writer which may provide helpful hints for the interpretation of the passage.

This study of the context of the preaching passage is especially important, since a text without a context will often result in being a pretext. The preacher should also recognize that if he is willing to spend more time in collecting Bible information, less time will be required later in preparing the actual sermon. Only the world was created *ex nihilo,* (out of nothing). Sermons are constructed out of subject matter. The preacher cannot preach the Bible until first of all he knows the Bible.

It is imperative that the biblical preacher maintain regular Bible study. He will want to develop a method for studying Bible books, chapters, paragraphs, doctrines, biographies, prayers, miracles, parables, and poetry. He may develop his own method, adopt the method followed by some other expositor, or follow methods advocated by such a book as *How to Search the Scriptures* by Culver and Perry.

COMMENTARIES AND STUDY BOOKS

It is necessary for the sermonizer to have books at his disposal which will provide help in the construction of sermons. At this point, we refer to those books which will assist him in obtaining background material and inspirational ideas which will prime the homiletical pump.

There are at least three types of commentaries. Each of these types serves a purpose for the preacher. The first type is that of the critical commentary. One of the best examples of this type is Keil & Delitzsch's work on the Old Testament. The second type is the homiletical commentary. One of these might be the *Pulpit Commentary,* and another might be Lange's work. This type of commentary provides some critical information but also gives some sermonic suggestions. The third type of commentary might be called the devotional. Matthew Henry's work would be an illustration of this type. Alexander Maclaren's commentary might also be listed as being devotional.

Some commentaries unfortunately do not provide material on the entire Bible. Often the portion on which the preacher desires help was omitted by that particular commentator. The beginning preacher will rely more heavily upon commentaries than the more experienced preacher.

When beginning one's preaching library, it is wise to purchase one set of homiletical commentaries covering the entire Bible. The preacher can then proceed to purchase commentaries on particular Bible books. Some preachers present series of messages on one Bible book or on a group of books. They then purchase several helpful works on that sections of the Bible. This specialization in purchasing books for immediate use protects the preacher's book budget.

Many books provide useful information for research projects but provide little assistance in stirring homiletical imagination and creativity. When giving consideration to the possible purchase of a book for a homiletical library, the preacher should find out if the author has had experience in preaching and therefore writes from the point of view of a preacher. Some books will often provide homiletical hints which may be studied in terms of critical data. Biblical and critical information without spiritual inspiration will tend to produce lectures rather than sermons. The preacher should remember that a sermon is not designed to be an essay in exegesis. Such preachers as G. Campbell Morgan, W. H. Griffith Thomas, F. B. Meyer, J. C. Massee, Lehman Strauss, W. A. Criswell, Charles L. Allen, Clovis G. Chappell, Clarence Macartney, W. Graham Scroggie, Guy King, Roy Laurin, and others have produced homiletically productive books.

Do not hesitate to read everything within your reach which has bearing upon the passage. It was Ernest Fremont Tittle who wrote, "If the church is empty it is largely because the preacher is empty."[7] The sermonizer should know far more about the portion of Scripture upon which the sermon is based than he is able to include within the sermon. This reading of material from extrabiblical sources should never be allowed to take the place of the exegetical study of the passage. Study the passage first and then read everything within reach.

### ANALYSIS OF THE CONTENT OF THE PREACHING PORTION

Having completed the first step in studying a preaching portion, which involves the survey of the context of the scriptural passage, the sermonizer proceeds to his second step, namely, the analysis of the content of the preaching portion. This involves several procedures. The first of these is to read the passage in several translations. Each time he reads the passage he pursues a different purpose in search of sermonic materials. The first reading should be made to determine the dominant impression gained from the passage. Having obtained this and written it on paper, so that it may not be lost, he turns to his second reading in order to discover the major and minor personages and that which is said about each one. After this material is recorded for further reference, he then turns to his third reading in order to note significant repeated words and phrases. If he has the original languages available for his use, it would be helpful to use either his

Greek or Hebrew at this reading. In the fourth reading, he seeks
to determine a distinctive name or title which may be given to
the passage as a means of identification. The fifth reading should
be done to prepare the passage for public reading from the pulpit. We suggest that the passage on which he is to preach should
be the passage that he reads as the scripture lesson in the main
portion of the worship service. Culver and Perry list the modern
translations together with an evaluation of each.[8]

After he has read the passage in several translations, he should
then proceed to formulate an analytical outline of the passage.
The paragraph divisions will indicate possible breaking points
for such an outline. As he makes this outline, no attempt should
be made to rearrange the order of contents within the passage.
Major and supporting ideas should be formulated in wording as
similar to that in the scripture passage as possible and arranged
so that a logical relationship is evident. The following writers
provide help in formulating such analytical outlines: Tenney,
Morgan, Thomas, Laurin, King, and Strauss.

The third procedure is to make a comparative study of parallel
passages. In doing this the preacher should note any significant
addition or deletion. This type of study will be especially relevant when preaching on the gospels. There is also a harmony by
Crockett in print covering the books of Samuel, Kings, and
Chronicles which may prove helpful.

A fourth procedure for analyzing the content of the preaching
portion is to make a grammatical survey. As he formulates the
grammatical survey, the sermonizer will proceed to diagram the
ideas within the passage after the manner used in diagramming
sentences. This will help to clarify the logical relationship between the ideas. This process is called thematic diagramming
and is illustrated by Culver and Perry.[9] In making the grammatical survey, the sermonizer will want to give special attention to
the pronunciation marks. These were not in the original manu-
scripts, but they have been added by translators to help convey
meaning and to clarify the series of declarations, explanations,
or questions. These may provide suggestions for preaching points
when it comes time to formulate the sermonic outline. The study
of the etymology of words will provide sermonic illustrative ma-

terial. The meaning of a word can be made more relevant by checking the connotation of the word. The context often clarifies the meaning of the word. Verb tenses should be noted since they have a greater significance in the Greek of the New Testament and the Hebrew of the Old Testament than they have in the general English translations. There are two translations which will help the student who at this point is handicapped by not knowing the original languages. One translation is that by Helen Montgomery entitled *The Centenary Translation of the New Testament*. The second translation, produced by John B. Williams, and titled *The New Testament,* is profitable to check the word order in the original language. In the Greek language, for instance, the emphatic words come first in the sentence. If the sermonizer does not have at hand a ready usage of the original languages, he may then profit by owning and using an interlinear Greek-English New Testament.

As the grammatical survey proceeds, the sermonizer will want to check the meaning of any figures of speech in the passage. These appear in abundance in the Scriptures, and each one within the particular preaching portion should be identified and clarified as to its meaning and implications. Repeated, peculiar, or distinctive terms may provide bases for sermon points in the construction of the outline itself.

## SEARCH FOR POSSIBLE SERMON IDEAS

The third step in studying a preaching portion beyond surveying the context and analyzing the content is that of searching the passage for possible sermon ideas. The sermonizer who has developed a homiletical mind will see far more possibilities for preaching within a given passage than one who is merely beginning to develop his sermonizing technique. The following hints or suggestions may prove helpful to the sermonizer as he surveys passages which may be profitable for sermonic development.

1. The sermonizer should ask first, whether the subject of the passage is developed in terms of one of the four following interrogative adverbs: why, how, when, or where. If so, then he has the first indication that it has possibilities for ser-

monic development by the modification process of sermon construction.

2. He may ask whether the subject of the passage is discussed from the standpoint of its nature. If so, he should develop the subject by the clarification process of sermon construction.

3. If there is a personal, community, or national problem cited, either directly or indirectly, a sermon could be developed that would seek a possible solution for that problem by the investigation process of sermon construction.

4. Sometimes a passage will include key words, or a key word indicator. A key word is a plural noun which may later characterize the main points of a message. Sample key words are *reasons, causes, effects, results,* and *ways.* If a key word such as *reasons* appears within the passage, and there are three or four reasons for believing or doing something, then this gives a hint that at a later time a message may be developed logically along these lines. There will be times when the key word itself may not be stated directly, but indicators may appear. For instance, though the key word *reasons* may not appear in that form, there may be a series of clauses beginning with wording such as *because of.* This will indicate that there are reasons included within the passage.

5. The sermonizer will want to discover the one main idea in each paragraph of the preaching portion. This main idea may provide the substance for the main point of a message or in some cases this main idea of the paragraph may provide the substance for the sermonic conclusion of a sermon to be developed.

6. If the passage deals with an incident, then the sermonizer may want to discover the steps involved in the unfolding of that incident. The steps may then provide bases for sermonic points.

7. Familiar verses within a passage may provide sermonic ideas. These are verses which have been known and appreciated by the people through the years. This fact may indicate that they are loaded with Biblical truth, and they may therefore have special sermonic possibilities.

8. If there is a particular figure of speech within the passage, the sermonizer will want to obtain a clear explanation of its meaning. He then may find that a message may be developed through the clarification of the meaning of that figure of speech showing its relationship to Christian living.
9. Cause and effect relationships within a passage may provide sermonic indicators.
10. A doctrinal emphasis within a passage may provide sermonic material.
11. The sermonizer will do well to ask whether there is an activity which is emphasized which should be performed or which should be avoided. If so, the sermon then may be developed showing why the activity should be performed or avoided.
12. Is there an emphasis within the passage upon a chronological or geographical order of events? Such may provide a series of times or places. These times or places may be the bases for sermon development.

As the sermonizer studies the passage for sermon ideas, he will do well to ask himself this question: What practical advice is there within this passage that will help me in daily living? Once the sermonizer finds within the passage that which has relevance for his daily living and that which grips his own soul, he will find it easier to share the truth of that passage with those to whom he will be speaking. He will then begin to sense that which prompted John Bunyan to say, "I preached what I felt; what I smartingly did feel." Both in preaching and in praying we should feel that there is something which must be declared.

Surely, few royal figures have crammed so much into so short a lifespan as King Edward VI of England, son of King Henry VIII. Born in 1537, he died in 1553, not quite sixteen. Certainly he must be one of the very few boys of whom a full-scale biography has been written! At nine years of age, on the occasion of his accession to the throne, he made history. On February 20, 1547, after the ceremony in Westminster Abbey, the boy king was walking in procession toward Westminster Hall where a banquet had been prepared. Just in front of him were officers of state bearing aloft three great swords. He asked what this meant,

and they told him that the swords stood respectively for each of
the three kingdoms under his crown. "One is wanting," he ex-
claimed, "the Bible, the sword of the Spirit!" And he ordered
that the large pulpit Bible should be taken from the lectern in
the abbey and carried with solemn dignity ahead of the symbols
of world power. Thus it comes about that to this day the presentation to the sovereign of a copy of the Word of God is part
of the English coronation service.[10]

One of the keys to revival is a return to preaching which is
saturated with the Word of God. In 2 Chronicles 34:15, we read,
"And Hilkiah answered and said to Shaphan the scribe, I have
found the book of the law in the house of the LORD." Following
this experience, a stirring from God came among the people.
There was evidence of a broken spirit (2 Ch 34:19), of a concerned spirit (2 Ch 34:21), and an obedient spirit (2 Ch 34:31),
wherein they determined to walk after the Lord and to keep His
commandments. We must help our people find the Word of the
Lord in the house of the Lord.

We should sift the Scriptures daily as did the Bereans in Acts
17:11. We should meditate upon the Scriptures as encouraged
by the psalmist in Psalm 1:2 and in Joshua 1:8. We should be
willing to accept the Word. "If any man will do his will, he
shall know of the doctrine, whether it be of God, or whether I
speak of myself" (Jn 7:17).

Let us not be like the hour glass which has the substance run
in and run out leaving nothing, nor like the sponge which takes
in and gives out without change, nor like the old-fashioned jelly
bag which kept in all the husks and allowed all the worthwhile
substance to get out. Be like the gold panner who with care and
patience sifts until the pure gold appears. Know the Word! Believe the Word! Obey the Word!

A cabman drove Charles Spurgeon home one day; and when
the great preacher paid his fare, the cabman said "A long time
since I drove you home, sir."

"But" said Spurgeon, "I don't remember you."

"Well," said the cabman, "I think it was about fourteen years
ago." He then pulled a worn and faded copy of the New Testament from his pocket, "Perhaps you remember this. You gave

it to me and asked me to read it, and I read it, and it led me to the Saviour, and I have been trying to serve Him through all these years."[11]

What a wonderful day it will be when they come to us and say, "I received the Word through your lips, I accepted Christ as Saviour and have tried to serve Him through the years."

## *Reading List*

Augustine, Aurelius. *On Christian Doctrine.* New York: Liberal Arts, 1958.

Blackwood, Andrew W. *The Preparation of Sermons.* Nashville: Abingdon-Cokesbury, 1946.

Broadus, John A. *A Treatise on the Preparation and Delivery of Sermons.* New York: Harper, 1944.

Gilkey, Langdon. *How the Church Can Minister to the World Without Losing Itself.* New York: Harper & Row, 1964.

Hoppin, James Mason. *The Office and Work of the Christian Ministry.* New York: Sheldon, 1869.

Hoyt, Arthur S. *The Work of Preaching.* New York: Macmillan, 1917.

Jordan, Gerald Ray. *You Can Preach.* New York: Revell, 1951.

Koller, Charles W. *Sermons Preached Without Notes.* Grand Rapids: Baker, 1964.

Perry, Lloyd M., and Culver, Robert D. *How to Search the Scriptures.* Grand Rapids: Baker, 1967.

Sanford, Jack D. *Make your Preaching Relevant.* Nashville: Broadman, 1963.

Sizoo, Joseph Richard. *Preaching Unashamed.* New York: Abingdon-Cokesbury, 1949.

Tittle, Ernest Fremont. *The Foolishness of Preaching.* New York: Henry Holt, 1930.

Turnbull, Ralph G., ed. *Baker's Dictionary of Practical Theology.* Grand Rapids: Baker, 1967.

Wagner, Don M. *The Expository Method of G. Campbell Morgan.* Westwood, N.J.: Revell, 1957.

Witherspoon, John. *Lectures on Moral Philosophy and Rhetoric.* Philadelphia: Woodward, 1810.

# 3

# Biblical Preaching
# and Its Logical Organization

IT IS AT THIS POINT that we might well ask, "Who is a great preacher?" That is a difficult question to answer. Time in some cases decreases the stamp of greatness placed upon him by his contemporaries. In other cases, a preacher gathering little attention in his own day is shown in the course of time to have left an important and indelible stamp upon the pages of history. We must also keep in mind the fact that greatness from man's viewpoint may be quite different from God's point of view.

Many preachers have been great in one particular aspect of the preaching task. Few have been great in many areas. If we are considering oratory, then we might list Robert Hall, Thomas Guthrie, George Whitefield, Thomas Chalmers, or Charles Haddon Spurgeon. If we are considering exposition, we might refer to Alexander Maclaren or Sir W. Robertson Nicoll. In respect to depth of thought, we might name Jonathan Edwards, Samuel Hopkins, or J. H. Newman. If we are looking for great preachers in terms of their teaching ability, then we might note Charles Simeon of Cambridge, Robertson of Brighton, or John Duncan of New College, Edinburgh. Great reformers might include the names of John Knox, Andrew Melville, or Thomas Boston. We might even list as one of the great preachers one who was raised in a gypsy tent and as an unlettered lad of seventeen preached his first sermon to a group of Sunday afternoon holidayers. He became an itinerant evangelist and preached before kings and queens before his death in 1947 at the age of eighty-seven years.

Five countries have wanted to claim him as their own. He was a converted gypsy they called Gipsy Smith.

Is a great preacher great because of the good organization of his message? Is he a great preacher providing he includes an abundance of scripture within his messages? Is he a great preacher because he is a deeply spiritual man?

Four tests for a great speech have come down to us from classical rhetoric. The Sophists, who were the first paid public speaking teachers, trained speakers to defend their position in the land courts of the island of Sicily. They felt that a speech was worthy of high commendation providing it *gained results.* Plato revolted against the position of the Sophists and emphasized the fact that a speech could only be considered great if it had *truth content.* The emphasis which Quintillian stressed was centered in the *inherent quality of life of the speaker.* A speech could only be termed a great speech providing it was delivered by a good man. The Aristotelian trademark of a great speech was that it be *well organized.* It is my feeling that all four of these emphases are worthy of recognition as we try to evaluate a sermon. We trust that through the guidance of the Holy Spirit that it will be used to produce constructive results. It certainly should convey truth. It should be presented by a man whose life is worthy. It is the fourth qualification of which this particular chapter is devoted. An effective biblical sermon should be marked by logical organization.

More than twenty men giving the Lyman Beecher Lectures on Preaching at Yale have discussed the organizing or arranging of the sermon for greater effectiveness. One of several significant comments was made by Kellman:

> The structure of the sermon may vary in many different ways, but the main point is that the sermon must have structure. It is true that only one or two of the hearers may recognize the presence or absence of structure for what it is; but they will all recognize the presence or absence of point, and point is the effect of structure.[1]

Many preachers must speak three or more times each week. Of course, preaching several sermons each week is not a new procedure. From the history of preaching we can note such examples

as that of John Wesley who between the experience at Alders-
gate and the time of his death preached an average of 16 sermons
a week for a total of 42,000.[2] Yet without a systematic approach
to sermonizing, not only will time be wasted but the preacher
will find an obvious tendency toward repetition and homiletical
frustration.

Following a systematic method for constructing a sermon does
not rule out nor does it limit the guidance of the Holy Spirit.
Orderliness, not confusion, is the evidence of the leading of the
Holy Spirit. He still, even as at creation, brings order out of
chaos.

This step-by-step procedure for constructing a sermon is an
attempt to find the message which is within the portion of Scripture and organize it in a manner which can be grasped by the
listener through the aid of the Holy Spirit.[3] The passage in the
Bible is not in the form of a sermon to be preached but is in a
form to be read. It is the aim of this procedure to keep the
message and meaning as it is but to put it into a form to be
preached.

Careful exegetical study should be given to the passage at
hand. When this material has been collected, the sermonizer is
encouraged to organize it around the theme of the passage. The
theme of the passage is the core of the sermon, the string which
joins the beads together. This approach might be termed "thematic biblical preaching." It organizes the material discovered
through exegesis into a form which is true to the message of the
passage and profitable for the listener.

## I. DETERMINE THE SUBJECT

The first step in constructing a biblical sermon is to *determine
the subject* of the sermon. The subject of the passage should
ideally be considered as the subject for the sermon. One of the
best ways to determine the subject of a passage and thus to discover the subject of the sermon to be constructed, is to read the
portion of scripture several times, while asking oneself this question: "What is the one main center of attention for this whole
passage?" Such a center of attention may be (1) a duty to per-
form; (2) a precept or a maxim to explore; (3) a problem to

solve; or, (4) an occupation, profession, or calling to pursue. Normally the subjects are given in terms of a single word or at most a short phrase. The passage for preaching should have as its subject, the matter of concern and importance which is relevant to the preaching purpose. It should capture the concern of the preacher in such a way that he feels that his listeners have a need for that subject. One of the tests of a sermon is that which happens to the man in the pew as a result of having heard that sermon. This subject represents a broad area out of which a number of themes may be selected for sermons. Here are a few examples of subjects which might serve as foundations for messages:

| | | |
|---|---|---|
| Affliction | Grace | Peace |
| Atonement | Heaven | Praise |
| Brotherhood | Hell | Prayer |
| Christ | Holiness | Sacrifice |
| The Church | Holy Spirit | Self-control |
| Courage | Judgment | Stewardship |
| Discipleship | Justification | Thanksgiving |
| Faith | Love | Work |
| Fear | Missions | Worship |
| Fellowship | Obedience | |
| Forgiveness | Patience | |

When the preacher has determined the subject of the preaching portion which in turn becomes the subject of his sermon, he will be wise at that point to gather information related to that subject. This process involves surveying the subject. When the sermonizer has answered the following ten questions, he will have accumulated an abundance of material. This will also provide helpful sermonic material when he comes to the actual writing of the sermon. These are the questions that he may well ask and answer:

1. What have I read on the subject?
2. What have I observed which may throw light upon the subject?
3. What have I gleaned from the experience of the past on the subject?

4. What is the actual meaning of the subject?
5. What does the Scripture have to say on the subject?
6. What is my personal attitude or bias toward the subject?
7. What is the attitude or bias of my congregation toward the subject?
8. What famous quotations can I remember or locate pertaining to this subject?
9. What poetry can I recall which is related to this subject?
10. What is the real importance of this subject at this particular time?

## II. Select the Theme

The second step in the formulation of a sermon is the selection of a *theme*. The theme of a sermon will be the particular aspect of the subject just discovered which is to be developed within this particular message. Each sermon has but one theme and one subject. It is the function of the theme to divide the subject and to suggest relationships. As the subject is normally one word, the theme will always be in the form of a phrase. It will be noted for brevity, clarity, and its comprehensiveness of the main thought of the sermon. The preacher should make certain that the subject selected in step one, and the theme selected here in step two, represent the subject and theme which is read out of the preaching portion rather than the subject and theme which the sermonizer reads into the preaching portion. It is at this point, especially in the construction of a sermon, that the sermonizer must guard against *eisegesis,* which is reading *into* a portion of Scripture as over against *exegesis,* which involves reading *out* of a passage of Scripture. Some examples might help to clarify what we are talking about:

1. If one's subject had been *prayer* in step one, then his theme here in step two might be "The profit of prayer."
2. If his subject in step one had been *God's work,* then his theme in step two might be "Supporting God's work."
3. If his subject had been *tithing* in step one, then his theme might be "The ability to tithe."

4. If his subject in step one had been *discouragement,* then the theme for step two might be "Overcoming discouragement."

Having selected the theme, the sermonizer should proceed to probe or survey the theme in order to collect material. In order to survey the theme, he should ask the following questions and proceed to answer them:

1. What was there in this preaching portion which led me to select this particular theme?
2. Are there terms in this theme which should be defined?
3. Are there similes and metaphors which would throw light upon the theme?
4. What is my personal relationship to this theme?
5. What relationship will the anticipated audience have to this theme?
6. What statements of Scripture will prove or strengthen this theme?
7. What relationship exists between each segment within the preaching portion and this particular theme?
8. Is this theme suitable for the time, place, and occasion on which I intend to preach the sermon?
9. Are there technical terms in the theme? If so, they should be explained and put into nontechnical form.
10. Finally, are there words in the theme which are employed in an unusual way?

### III. FORMULATE A PROPOSITION

The third step in the construction of a sermon is the formulation of a *proposition.* The proposition occupies the focal point in the sermon outline. This part of the sermon has been referred to by different homiletical writers as the central idea, the controlling assertion, the statement, the big truth, the subject sentence, and the thesis. It is this sentence which is the integrating center of the sermon. It promotes stability of structure, unity of thought, and forcefulness of impact. It proclaims the truth which the sermonizer desires to establish and apply. The proposition announces the theme in sentence form. It should embody the principal or most striking truth of the scriptural portion on which the man is preaching. It is important that this sentence be true to the impact of Scripture and also that it be relevant to human experience. Great preaching should be in the present tense. It must speak to the concerns of the day and in the thought forms and language of that day. The proposition, in other words, must be stated in the form of a timeless truth which was valid for Bible times and is still valid for the day in which it is being preached. Since it is a timeless truth, no proper names other than that of deity should be included within it. There are three types of propositions from which the sermonizer may choose: (1) *a statement of evaluation or judgment:* "Praying is profitable"; (2) *a statement of obligation or duty:* "It is necessary for Christians to engage in intercessory prayer,'" or "Christians should support God's work"; (3) *a statement of activity without stated obligation:* "We *can* become more effective in praying," or "Every Christian *can* tithe," or "A Christian *can* overcome discouragement." In the third type of proposition, the emphasis is placed upon *ability*.

## IV. Establish a Transitional Sentence

The fourth step in the construction of a sermon is the establishing of a *transitional sentence*. At this point in our sermon construction we are ready to establish a rhetorical bridge between the core of the sermon, which is the proposition, and the development of the sermon, which is found in the body of the message. This rhetorical bridge is in the form of a transitional sentence which gathers within it that which has preceded and makes a logical transition to that which is to follow.

Having established the proposition for the sermon under construction in the preceding step, the sermonizer now applies one of the six following questions to the proposition. The body of the sermon should answer that question for the listener. His selection of one of these six questions will depend upon the content of the preaching portion and the emphasis that is found within it. The six possible questions from which he will choose *one* are the following:

|                  |                  |
|------------------|------------------|
| *How* can I?     | *Where* should I? |
| *Why* should I?  | *Where* can I?   |
| *When* should I? | *Why* is it?     |

One of these six questions should serve to guide the thinking of the sermonizer in terms of the development of the particular message on which he is preaching. Notice that there are four interrogative adverbs included within these six questions. Those four interrogative adverbs are *how, why, when,* and *where.* Probably 75 percent of the messages preached by the average sermonizer can be classified as sermons which answer either how, why, when, or where in respect to the proposition. This transitional sentence which he is seeking to establish in our present step has three parts:

One of these three parts is the *sermonic interrogative.* This is the one interrogative adverb which the sermonizer has selected out of the four.

The second part of the transitional sentence is the *proposition* in as complete a form as possible. This proposition is that which he formulated in step three.

There is still a third item to be discovered and incorporated within the transitional sentence. This third item is a *key word.* The key word is a noun. It is always in the plural. It characterizes the main points of the message. A single sermon has only one key word, and that key word will always appear within the transitional sentence. It should be noted at this point that it never appears in the proposition of the sermon constructed according to this basic pattern. There are many key words from which the sermonizer may select one for a given sermon. Take note of the plural nouns which appear in the following word groupings, thus seeing how a key word can appear in a sermonic setting. If the interrogative in your sermon were *why,* then you might use the following:

> because of *arguments* set forth
> because of *benefits* to be derived
> because of *commands* that are given
> because of *guarantees* provided
> because of *incentives* offered
> because of *invitations* extended
> because of *joys* to be realized
> because of *profits* to be gained

> because of *reasons* set forth
> because of *values* to be realized

Of course, this list is by no means exhaustive. It is only suggestive.

If the interrogative adverb in the sermon were *how,* then note a few of the possible words in sermonic setting:

> by following *instructions*
> by surmounting *obstacles*
> by heeding *admonitions*
> by avoiding *dangers*
> by obeying *directives*
> by following the *steps*
> by practicing the *lessons*
> by avoiding *mistakes*
> by taking advantage of the *powers*
> by heeding the *precautions*
> by making use of *provisions*
> by following the *rules*

The key word in each phrase is the plural noun.

If the interrogative adverb were *where,* then he might discuss areas, places, locations, regions. By using a dictionary of synonyms and *Roget's Thesaurus,* the sermonizer will keep expanding the list of these plural nouns. He will find it profitable to repeat the list of key words until he becomes well acquainted with them. This is a profitable step in developing the homiletical mind. When this happens he will find himself reading a passage of Scripture and spotting these words. When it comes time to sermonize, these key words will lead him to discover main points for his message.

Having located the three parts of a transitional sentence, namely, an *interrogative adverb,* a *proposition,* and a *key word,* which is a plural noun, the sermonizer now faces the task of putting these three elements together in good English sentence form. As he proceeds to do this, he will discover on occasion that instead of using an *interrogative adverb,* that it may be advantageous for him to use an *interrogative substitute* in order to facilitate the flow of the English sentence. We therefore have established acceptable interrogative substitutes for the simple interrogative adverbs. If the interrogative adverb for a given message is *how,* then if the flow of the English in the transitional sentence needs to be improved, the sermonizer may use in place of *how* the preposition *by* followed by a verb ending in *ing.* For example, *by obeying* would be the form of the interrogative substitute. If the sermonic interrogative *why* and the flow of the English in the transitional sentence could be improved by the use of a substitute, then the acceptable substitute is *because of* followed by the key word. If the sermon interrogative is *when* or *where* then the acceptable substitutes are *in which* or *at which.*

We now turn to an example of the actual transitional process involved in forming a transitional sentence having been given a *proposition.* This transitional process does not appear on the sermon outline but should be employed by the sermonizer. The proposition might read: "A nation can become prosperous." The sermonizer then precedes that proposition with an interrogative adverb such as *how,* thereby formulating a question: "How can a nation become prosperous?" He then answers that question by selecting a key word and putting that key word into a phrase. That phrase might read "by obeying commands." He has now taken his *proposition,* applied an *interrogative adverb* to it, thus making the proposition into the form of a question, and has answered that question with a *key word.* He now proceeds to put these three parts (the key word, the interrogative or interrogative substitute, and the proposition) into one sentence called the transitional sentence. This could be his transitional sentence: "A nation can become prosperous by observing the commands of God."

There is one additional element which he may want to add to his transitional sentence. If the sermon is constructed upon one particular passage of Scripture, he may want to add the designation of the preaching portion at the close of the transitional sentence. If he does, then the transitional sentence would read in is entirety: "A nation can become prosperous by obeying the commands of God, as set forth in Deuteronomy 6:1-25."

Let us analyze the transitional sentence for its parts. The

phrase "by obeying" is the *interrogative substitute* for the interrogative "how." The "commands of God" represents the *key
phrase* including the key word "commands." "A nation can
become prosperous" is the *proposition*. Deuteronomy 6:1-25 is
the designation of the preaching portion upon which the sermon
is based. A sample sermon outline based upon this passage is
located at the end of this chapter.

Having used Deuteronomy 6:1-25 as our preaching portion,
we would suggest the following four parts of a possible sermon
outline covering the theory presented up to this point.

The sermon *subject:*          *Prosperity.*
The sermon *theme:*            *How to become prosperous.*
The *proposition:*             *A nation can become prosperous.*
The *transitional sentence:* A nation can become prosperous *by
                               obeying* the *commands of God* as
                               set forth in Deuteronomy 6:1-25.

We have given consideration to the first four steps in the formulation of the sermon outline. These steps are the following:

    1.  Determine the subject.
    2.  Formulate the theme.
    3.  Construct a proposition.
    4.  Establish a transitional sentence.

It may be well at this point to give some examples of these four
steps as they are synchronized.

*Example One.* If the subject of a message were *soul-winning*
and the theme "The necessity for soul-winning," then the proposition might be "Every Christian should be a soul-winner." The
transitional sentence would then read: "Because of the following reasons every Christian should be a soul-winner."

*Example Two.* If the subject of the message were *tithing* and
the theme "The ability to tithe," then the proposition might
read: "Every Christian can tithe." The transitional sentence
might read: "By following the procedures set forth in this
passage, every Christian can tithe."

*Example Three.* If the subject were *prayer* and the theme

"Places to Pray," the proposition might read: "Christians should Pray" and the transitional sentence, "There are several places in which Christians should pray."

*Example Four.* If the subject of the message were *waiting on the Lord,* the theme might be: "The wisdom of waiting on the Lord"; the proposition: "It is wise to wait upon the Lord." And the transitional sentence: "Because of the following reasons it is wise to wait upon the Lord."

*Example Five.* If the subject of the message were *prayer* and the theme "When to Pray," the proposition might read: "Christians should pray," and the transitional sentence might be: "There are several times in which Christians should pray."

## V. DEVELOP MAIN DIVISIONS

The fifth step in the sermonic process is that of developing *main divisions.* Dr. John Watson, better known as Ian Maclaren, once said, "Whether . . . a sermon ought to be parcelled out into heads is an important question. Three detached sermonettes do not make one sermon; but, on the other hand, a handful of observations tied together by a text are not an organic whole. It all depends on whether the heads advance, ascend, cumulate, or are independent, disconnected, parallel."[4]

The main divisions in a sermon serve to amplify, explain, or prove the proposition. Normally there will not be more than five, and never less than two main divisions. If more than five were used, neither the preacher nor his congregation could remember them. The sermonizer will seek to make the points clear and concise in construction as well as in presentation. He must bear in mind the fact that the listener must note the points, ponder them, and remember them. The form and content of the main points of a message will be controlled by the key word, and all of the main points within a message are characterized by that key word.

There are certain rules of grammar and structure which should be observed in the formulation of the main points of a message. It would be wise to have the main divisions in parallel grammatical form whenever possible. It is wise to avoid figurative language in stating the main points since such language is

ambiguous. The points should be arranged with the listeners
in mind to whom they are presented. The purpose behind the
presentation will also have an influence upon their order. Visual
memory of the preacher will be aided as he underlines the main
points on his sermon outline.

The sermonizer should bear in mind the fact that the thoroughly biblical sermon will find its main points within the
passage upon which the preacher is preaching. Since they come
directly from the Scripture, he should place what we term a scriptural undergirding at the end of each main point. This scriptural undergirding consists of the notation of the Bible book,
chapter, and verse reference which substantiates the main point.
That part of the verse should be written after the reference
which says biblically that which the main point states. It should
be noted that in the sample sermon based upon Deuteronomy 6,
the passage itself highlights the fact that the main points should
be considered, since they are "commands" or "commandments"
of God. In Deuteronomy 6:25, we read: "And it shall be our
righteousness, if we observe to do all these commandments before the Lord our God, as He hath commanded us." Now let
us state four commands which might represent the four main
points found in this particular passage.

1. *Remember God.* (v. 12) : "Then beware lest thou forget the
   Lord."
2. *Love God.* (v. 5) : "And thou shalt love the Lord thy God."
3. *Declare God.* (vv. 6-7a) : "And these words, which I command
   thee this day, shall be in thine heart: and thou shalt teach
   them diligently."
4. *Serve God.* (v. 13) : "Thou shalt fear the Lord thy God, and
   serve him."

Take note of the fact that these main points do not have to
be arranged in order exactly as they appear in Scripture, but
rather they can be arranged in view of the particular emphasis
which the preacher feels led to make in this particular message.
When the sermonizer finds his main points within a given passage and specifies the chapter and verse reference after each, the
listeners will thereby be encouraged to note the points within

their Bible. This will put them in form for reference at a later time.

## VI. Amplify the Main Divisions

The sixth step involves the amplifying of the main divisions into *subdivisions*. These are sometimes referred to as subpoints. At other times, they are referred to as arabics. Amplification is the functional process of obtaining subdivisions which will amplify and explain the main points of the message. There will be at least two and normally not more than five of these subdivisions under each main point. Since it is desired that these subdivisions as well as the main points under which they are listed are to be remembered by the listener, it is important that they be (1) short in form, (2) few in number, and (3) similar in structure. As many of the subdivisions as possible should be drawn from the passage upon which the sermonizer is basing his message.

The simplest method of getting subdivisions under the main points is to take one of the six interrogative words (how, why, when, where, who, or what) and apply this word to the main point. A question will thus result which the subdivision can then answer. More than one subdivision may be gleaned by applying a single interrogative word to the main point.

Subdivisions may be obtained by making an exposition of the main point. This may take the form of exposition by definition. One may define by giving synonyms, putting the item in its correct classification, giving the etymology of a word, or by telling what the main point is not, which is defining by negation.

The main point may also be amplified by narration. This is the functional process of presenting a series of events in story form. These may be illustrations of the main divisions. It will involve putting into word-picture form persons and objects, thus telling how persons or things look, feel, or act. If the main division is an incident, it may be unfolded by following these four steps: (1) establish the setting and get the action started; (2) develop the main body of the incident; (3) bring the incident to its logical climax; (4) draw the conclusion which may well be a logical application for the listener.

A main point can sometimes be developed by using the process of thought categorization, as set forth by A. E. Garvie in his book *The Christian Preacher.* There are certain patterns of thinking which when recognized and followed will aid in establishing a logical unfolding of an idea.[5] If the main point, for instance, involves a *person,* then this person may be sketched as to heredity, environment, development, capacity, character, career, achievement, and reputation. If the main point were an *event,* then the sermonizer might examine the event in regard to time, place, antecedents, consequences, human participation, and evidences of divine providence. If the main point involves *relationships,* these relationships might be itemized as being in relation to self, neighbor, and to God. The *time* order may be used to show the relation to the past, present, and the future. If one were considering an incident such as a biblical miracle of healing, he might survey the case, cause, cure, and consequence. A *category of size* or dimension involves breadth, length, depth, and height. The category of *spiritual status* might include saints, sinners, preconversion, and post-conversion. The *spiritual development* category might be formulated and include the call, conduct, and compensation.

In addition to these general methods, there are two additional suggestions which may be noted in connection with the formulation of subpoints in a message. First, it will be helpful to define any words within the main point which need definition, and this would be well to do in the first subdivision. This will mean that the listener knows the meaning of that main point immediately after it has been given. The final suggestion pertains to the application in connection with each main division. It is recommended that at least the last subpoint of the main point be a subpoint of application. This application points out specific ways in which the main point may be applied to the living experience of the listener. It is our feeling that the present day congregation will not wait for the application until the conclusion of the message. The congregation demands that the main emphasis of the message be applied point by point. American preachers have traditionally waited until the last part of the message to add the application. British preachers tend to put applications throughout the sermon. I feel that the British method is to be preferred.

## VII. Formulate an Introduction

The seventh step involves the formulation of an *introduction.* The introduction is that part of the sermon which clarifies the reason for that particular audience to listen to that particular preacher discuss that particular subject on that occasion. It is composed of three parts:

Part one is the *approach sentence.* In formulating the approach sentence, the sermonizer should select a word or idea within the proposition which needs definition, clarification, or amplification. This word or idea will become the core of the approach sentence and will also become the core of the remaining portion of the introduction. This core thought of the introduction should be developed in terms of the daily living of the listeners. We should like to emphasize the practicality of the statement by Phillips Brooks who said, "A good sermon meets the listeners where they are, and leaves them at the foot of the cross." This means to us that the sermon should begin with a secular discussion of the word or phrase selected from the proposition.

The second part of the introduction is the *outlined portion,* which consists of the development of the approach sentence in outline form.

Part three of the introduction is termed the *sermonic explanation.* It is inserted within the sermon outline as the final segment of the introduction. It is the sermonic bridge between the secular segment of the introduction and the body of the sermon which is to follow. This explanation will put the sermon into its biblical setting. This explanation will also include any unique features of the particular type of sermon which is to be presented. It will help the listener prepare to follow the sermonic development in his Bible.

The complete introduction should occupy no more than 15 percent of the speaking time for the entire message. It should be marked by such characteristics as brevity, clarity, appropriateness, unification, purposefulness, variety, and audience interest. It should be presented in a friendly, tactful, and direct manner in order to stimulate the listener's interest. Such items as flattery, apologies, and items of complexity should be avoided. Technical language within the introduction will tend to short-circuit the listening of the audience. It is not wise in the first part of the message to reveal the main points of the sermon which are to come. Any material, whether humorous or serious, which is not relevant to the sermon at hand should be avoided. The introduction is not an end in itself, but points to that which is to come.

## VIII. FORMULATE A CONCLUSION

The eighth step in the writing of a sermon is the formulation of the conclusion. The conclusion is the summarization of the sermon showing its relevance to the daily living of the listeners. It will challenge the listeners to make some decision regarding the content of the message. A conclusion has two parts.

The first of these is the objective sentence which is the first sentence of the conclusion. It is formulated by beginning with the words, "Therefore, we should." This introduction to the conclusion will be followed by the particular response desired by the speaker to the message. The objective sentence is sometimes referred to as the proposition plus purpose.

This objective sentence is then followed by an outlined section. This outlined section may consist of a recapitulation of the main points or a restating of the applications that have been made throughout the sermon. This may be paraphrased or put into epigrammatic form. The sermonizer may choose to list a series of specific ways in which the suggested applications made within the sermon can be specifically applied to the lives of the listeners. He may want to challenge the hearers to accept the points made within the message through appealing to altruism, aspiration, curiosity, duty, fear, love, or reason. Charles Koller, in his book *Expository Preaching Without Notes,* refers to these as the seven basic appeals.[6] If the main points of the message have been stated as negatives, the preacher should then use a positive conclusion for his message. The message should be concluded on a positive note. If the preacher is aware of the fact that several who are listening may be erecting within their minds certain objections to giving a favorable response to his message, he may want to list those anticipated objections and provide a positive answer for each, rather than allowing the listener to establish these in his thinking as unanswered mental objections.

The conclusion should be concise. If it is too long, interest will tend to lag. No material should be inserted which is not relevant to the main thrust of the message. The conclusion is not the place for an apology, joke, or humorous remark. It is not necessary, nor is it wise to give a formal statement to the listener that the conclusion is now approaching.

Prepare the conclusion with care, and make certain that it is a conclusion for that specific message rather than one of broad generalities.

## IX. The Addition of Illustrative Material

Having completed the eight specific steps in the formulation of a sermon outline, the preacher should now turn to some general items involved in the sermon process. The first of these is the addition of the illustrative material where it is needed for throwing light on the contents of the message. Only one illustration should be used for a single idea. The illustrative material should be relevant, plausible, and in good taste. Different types of illustrations should be used. These illustrations should be gathered from a variety of sources.

Different preachers have different methods for collecting illustrative material. In fact we might list six of the more popular methods. Some store them in books of one's occasional thoughts and favorite quotations. These books are referred to as "commonplace books." This was Brooks' method. Spurgeon encouraged his students to follow the same practice lest they run the risk of becoming commonplace themselves. W. E. Sangster added the warning, however, that to put illustrations within a commonplace book in an unclassified manner would make the "book no better than a bin."

D. L. Moody used the method of storing illustrations in envelopes. Such envelopes often wear out too soon or are mislaid or lost. A. T. Pierson, Henry Sloane Coffin, and Leslie Weatherhead used a filing cabinet for the storage of their illustrations. It was the practice of W. L. Watkinson and Frank W. Boreham to store their illustrations in their memory. D. C. Bryan found that it was practical to clip the illustrations and store them in scrapbooks. Sangster employed the method of storing his illustrations in libraries. He would underline or in some way mark the illustration. On blank pages at the end of the book or on the inside cover, he would identify such illustrations and the pages where they might be found. One of the great difficulties with this method is found in the fact that the library is not always available.

There are some of us who do not have formal files of illustrations. An illustration is located for a particular sermon and is then used only in that sermon. One great danger of having a file of illustrations is found in the tendency to use an illustration over and over again.

Some of the sources for illustrative material include the Bible, personal observation, personal experience, literature, hymns, art, imagination, history, missions, comparative religions, athletics, science, travel, and hobbies. It was Spurgeon's feeling, however, that there were no illustrations as good as those taken from Scripture.

## X. The Formulation of a Title

The sermonizer will want to formulate a title which should be selected in keeping with the mood of the sermon, the nature of the audience, and the content of the message. It should not contain more than four thought-carrying words. This title should provide bulletin board appeal. It will also provide a means for filing the message after it has been presented.

## The Arrangement of the Sermon Items

The preacher is now ready to arrange the items which have been formulated into the form of a sermon outline covering one side of an 8½-by-11 sheet of paper. In this written outline he needs only four complete sentences. These four sentences will be the approach sentence, the proposition, the transitional sentence, and the objective sentence. He should make use of abbreviations wherever possible and should only use as many words as are absolutely necessary. The sermon outline should not demand more than one side of the 8½-by-11-inch sheet of paper. If the preacher should need to take his outline into the pulpit, he will then never have to turn a sheet of  paper while he is preaching.


## BASIC SERMON PATTERN

PREACHING PORTION: Deuteronomy 6:1-25

SERMONIC PROCESS: Modification

SUBJECT: Prosperity

THEME: How to Become Prosperous


### Obedience Brings Prosperity

INTRODUCTION

*Approach Sentence:* Prosperity has its price.

*Outlined Portion*

    1. Prosperity: "A thriving condition, good fortune, success."

    2. "Watch lest prosperity destroy generosity." H. W. Beecher

*Explanation*

    1. (Show that the subject and theme of the sermon are inherent within the preaching portion.)

    2. (Point out features of the content and context of the preaching portion which may have interest value as far as the theme is concerned.)

    3. (Show the significance of the type of sermon as related to Scripture, the occasion and the congregation.)

PROPOSITION: A nation can become prosperous.

TRANSITIONAL SENTENCE: A nation can become prosperous by obeying the commandments of God as set forth in Deuteronomy 6:1-25.

MAIN DIVISIONS

    I. *Remember God* (v. 12): "Then beware lest thou forget the LORD."

        1. (Each subpoint is related to the main point under which it is

        2. listed. It does not refer to the preceding subpoint.)

        3.

        4. (Subpoint of application.)

           (Illustration: Danger of Prosperity)

II. *Love God* (v.5): "And thou shalt love the LORD thy God."

    1. (As far as possible, undergird each subpoint with Scripture.)
    2.
    3. (Subpoint of application.)
       (Illustration: Song: Love of God.)

III. *Declare God* (vv. 6-7a): "And these words, which I command thee this day, shall be in thine heart: and thou shalt teach them diligently."

    1.
    (Illustration: Tephilim)
    2.
    3.
    4.
    5. (Subpoint of application.)

IV. *Serve God* (v. 13): "And thou shalt fear the LORD thy God, and serve him."

    1.
    2.
    (Illustration: Exodus 17:1-7)
    3. (Subpoint of application.)

CONCLUSION: Therefore, we as a nation should seek to become prosperous. Deuteronomy 6:25: "And it shall be our rigteousness, if we observe to do all these commandments before the LORD our God, as he hath commanded us."

1. *Remember God.*      3. *Declare God.*
2. *Love God.*          4. *Serve God.*

Most of the preacher's sermons will be preached using this basic preaching plan which we have discussed up to this point. We noted earlier that probably 75 percent of his sermons will employ the process of modification. He should, however, have available for the other 25 percent of his sermons some additional methods as needed for the exposition of unique types of biblical content.

The analogy might be drawn between the sermonizer and the baseball pitcher. The baseball pitcher may have as his basic pitch a fast ball. If he is wise, he will seek to develop one or two other types of pitches in order that in the course of the game, he may alter the pitches, thereby keeping the batter challenged by change. The sermonizer should likewise vary the types of sermons preached in order that the listeners will be kept on the alert at all times. This variation will not only stimulate interest on the part of the listener, but will stir up creativeness within the mind and heart of the preacher. It will also do more complete justice to the varying types of Scripture to be expounded. Variety is a necessary ingredient of effective preaching; we do not strive for variety for its own sake, but rather to enhance communication.

Good ideas are abundant, but the art of organizing them is not as common. Organization is a creative process; therefore, it may be approached in different ways. When the sermonizer desires to organize his thoughts into sermonic form, he should first determine the purpose, then decide upon the plan, and finally develop the process.

## SERMON PROCESS INDICATORS

How can the sermonizer discover which sermon process to use for a given sermon on a given passage? Should he use the process of modification, which involves the basic sermon plan? Or should he use this process of clarification, which we are to discuss? He will always try to use the modification process as his basic preaching plan whenever possible. He will only use the clarification process when the passage and the purpose behind his sermon demand it. There are certain indicators which may help him identify a passage as being one especially adapted to this process.

The first of these indicators is the presence of an *analogy* within the passage. This analogy may be developed and amplified in such a way that the sermonizer can clarify the meaning of a spiritual concept for his listeners.

A second indicator is that of the presence of an *important English Bible word* within the particular preaching passage or a series of scriptural passages. This word when clarified in meaning by checking the Greek and Hebrew origins could provide the listener with a more comprehensive understanding of the breadth of meaning of the concept represented by that one English word.

The third indicator is the reference within the passage to a *doctrine,* the meaning of which could be clarified by showing evidences of its application to daily life. This reference to a doctrine within the passage may involve a direct affirmation within the Scripture itself or it may involve a doctrinal statement formulated by the sermonizer which is based upon the teaching of the passage.

A fourth indicator is that of the presence of a statement of *principle* within the passage the meaning of which can be amplified and clarified by giving a series of illustrations of its truth to the listener.

A fifth indicator is the presence of an extremely significant *verse of scripture,* the words and phrases of which carry implications and inferences which when amplified will help the listener grasp the importance and depth of meaning within that verse of scripture.

A sixth indicator is the presence of the *account of an incident* or the elaboration of a process within the passage of Scripture, which when clarified as to its parts or steps involved, will help the listener to grasp and understand the spiritual truth that the experience or process was meant to impart.

The seventh indicator involves the reference to a *group of individuals.* The specific identification of these individuals will help to make the passage more meaningful as a sermonic base.

In our discussion of the modification sermonic process, we noted the fact that each sermon must have a key word (a noun in the plural) which would characterize the main points of the message. This is also true of the sermons written by the process of clarification. If the passage contains the first indicator, namely an analogy, then the sermon will develop comparisons or similarities. If the passage emphasizes a word study, then the sermon will elaborate definitions of an English Bible word. If a doctrinal declaration is to be used as a basis for the sermon, then the main points will be evidences or applications of that doctrinal declaration. If the fourth indicator is used as a basis for the sermon, then the main points will be illustrations of the principle. If the fifth indicator is used, namely an extremely significant verse of Scripture, then the main points will be either implications or inferences gleaned from the words and phrases within that verse. If the sixth indicator is used (an incident or process), then the main points will be parts of that incident or steps with the process. If the seventh indicator is used (a group of people), then the main points will involve the identification of specific individuals within the group.

We are dealing therefore at this point with seven different types of biblical content which normally will indicate the advisability of using the process of clarification.

The eight steps which were used in connection with the basic preaching plan of modification will be used for the construction of sermons for clarification. These same eight steps should be followed in sequence.

## SERMON TYPES INVOLVING
## THE CLARIFICATION PROCESS

1. Analogy or Comparison

   By developing an *analogy* within Scripture, I can clarify the meaning of a spiritual concept. (Key words: *Comparisons* or *Similarities*)

2. Biblical Word

   By providing *definitions* for a significant *English Bible word,* I can clarify the fullness of its meaning. (Key word: *Definitions*)

3. Doctrinal Statement

   By giving *evidences* of the application of a *doctrinal affirmation* to daily life, I can clarify the signifance of the doctrinal declaration. (Key words: *Evidences* or *Applications*)

4. Statement of Principle

   By giving a series of *illustrations,* I can clarify the meaning and enforce the truth of the *statement of principle.* (Key word: *Illustrations*)

5. Scripture Verse

   By drawing *implications* or *inferences* from words or phrases within a verse of scripture, I can clarify and amplify the meaning of that *verse.* (Key words: *Implications* or *Inferences*)

6. An Experience

By going through the *parts* of an *experience* or the *steps* of a *process,* I can clarify the relationship between each of these and the spiritual timeless theme which the incident was meant to convey. (Key words: *Parts* or *Steps*)

7. Identities

By giving specific identification of *individuals* referred to collectively in the proposition, I can clarify the extent of personal involvement in connection with the *duty, doctrine, precept, problem, occupation, profession,* or *calling.* (Key word: *Individuals*)

## CLARIFYING AN ANALOGY OR COMPARISON

The first sermon type involving the process of clarification is that which involves the developing of an analogy or comparison. There are two passages of Scripture which we will use for examples. The first of these is Hebrews 12:1-17. A sample sermon outline based upon this passage is located near the end of this chapter. The subject for the sermon based upon this passage might be "Living the Christian Life." The theme might be "Comparisons between living the Christian life and running a race." (Note that the key word *comparisons,* which is a noun in the plural, appears within the theme for the sermon). The proposition for the sermon might be: "Living the Christian life is like running a race." The proposition is, therefore, a simple statement of the analogy which is to be developed later within the sermon. The transitional sentence for this sermon might read, "The following comparisons between living the Christian life and running a race will help to clarify how we ought to live the Christian life." The key word *comparisons* appears within the transitional sentence.

There should be no question in the mind of the listener, but that this sermon is aimed at clarifying this concept of how to live the Christian life by developing the analogy between living the Christian life and running a race. A sample main point for this sermon might read: "Just as it is wise to avoid hindrances when one is running a race, so it is wise to avoid hindrances when one is living a Christian life." When preaching on Hebrews 12, the points for the message can be gleaned from the scriptural passage itself. This is not true of our next example.

Let us now turn to the second passage, Matthew 5:13. In this case, the main points are not included within the preaching message. There is only the statement of the analogy. In this case main points must be derived by developing the secular item within the analogy and then seeking to find spiritual implications. The subject for this sermon on Matthew 5:13 might be "The nature of the Christian life." The theme might read: "Comparisons between the nature of the Christian life and the nature of salt." The proposition involves the simple statement of the analogy: "The nature of the Christian life is like the nature of salt." The transitional sentence might read: "The following comparisons between the nature of the Christian life and the nature of salt will help clarify what our Christian life should be like." The key word "comparisons" appears in the transitional sentence just as it appeared in the theme. A sample main point for such a method might read, "As salt acts to stop the spread of physical decay, so the Christian should be a force to stop the spread of spiritual decay."

Within the main points for such a message, there is first the physical portion of the analogy followed by the spiritual aspect of the analogy. The sermonizer may find it helpful, therefore, to use the first subpoint under each main point to develop the physical aspect of the main point, and the second subpoint to develop the spiritual aspect. The third subpoint could then emphasize the practical application of the main point.

The introduction for this type of message which develops an analogy might stress the significance of the physical part of the analogy in the life of the past and the present.

### CLARIFYING A BIBLICAL WORD

The second type of sermon aims at clarifying biblical truth by providing definitions for a significant English Bible word. In order to illustrate this sermon type, let us take the word "forgiveness." A sample sermon outline of this type of sermon is located near the end of this chapter. Forgiveness is the subject of the sermon. The theme would read: "Definitions of forgiveness."

The key word "definitions" appears in the statement of the theme. The proposition for such a sermon might read: "God forgives sin." The transitional sentence might be stated: "A study of the definition of the English Bible word *forgiveness* will help clarify what is involved in God's forgiving sin." A sample main point for such a message might read: "The English Bible word *forgive* in Psalm 78:38 is the word *kophar* meaning to cover."

Subpoints for such a message would include a discussion of the word picture behind the Greek or Hebrew and also, references to the occurrence and significance of the word in Scripture and its application to the daily life of the listener.

### CLARIFYING A DOCTRINAL DECLARATION

The third sermon type has for its purpose the clarification of a doctrinal declaration by giving evidences or applications of its truth in daily life. As an example for this type of sermon let us turn to Jonah 1. This passage might have as its subject: "The sovereignty of God." This is a good place for us to emphasize the fact that the subject of the chapter should be the subject of the sermon. The theme would be "Evidences of the sovereignty of God." The proposition might read, "God is sovereign." The transitional sentence for such a sermon might read: "A study of the evidences of God's sovereignty will help to clarify the practical value of this doctrinal truth." A sample main point might read: "The doctrinal teaching that God is sovereign is evidenced in His designation of His workers." In this particular sermon the doctrinal truth "God is sovereign" is not specifically stated within the passage. The sermonizer formulates the truth on the strength of the content and doctrinal emphasis of the passage.

### CLARIFYING A STATEMENT OF PRINCIPLE

The fourth sermon type involves the clarification of the meaning of a statement of principle by giving illustrations of that principle which will visualize and apply its truth. For example, we might use Numbers 32:23, which reads, "Be sure your sin will find you out." The subject for this sermon might be "The certainty of sin's discovery." The theme for such a message, "Illustrations of the principle that it is certain that sin will be discovered." The key word introduces the sermon theme. The next step is to formulate the proposition. The proposition for this type of sermon might read: "It is certain that sin will be discovered." The proposition is then a declarative statement of principle. It has put the subject into sentence form. The transitional sentence is introduced by the key word and might read: "Illustrations of the principle that it is certain that sin will be discovered as set forth in Numbers 32:23 will help impress this truth upon us." Each main point of this sermon will be based upon an illustration which when presented to the congregation will emphasize the truth of the proposition. This type of sermon clarifies a verse of Scripture by giving several illustrations of the one truth. It impresses through repetition. Some might refer to it as being an impressionistic sermon.

### Clarifying the Meaning of a Verse of Scripture

The fifth type of sermon in the clarification process takes a verse of Scripture and clarifies its meaning by drawing implications and inferences from its words and phrases. The sermonizer must first of all determine the subject of the verse which will also be the subject of the sermon. If we were to formulate a sermon using Psalm 46:1, "God is our refuge and strength, a very present help in trouble," our subject might be "God's provision for us." The theme might read: "Implications of the verse, 'God is our refuge and strength, a very present help in trouble,' as these help us understand God's provision for us." The proposition might read: " 'God is our refuge and strength, a very present help in trouble,' can help us understand God's provision for us." The transitional sentence would be: "The implications drawn from the words and phrases of this verse of Scripture can help us understand God's provision for us." Each main point of the message will contain an implication drawn from a word or phrase in the scripture verse which helps us understand God's provision for us.

### Clarifying the Meaning of an Experience

The sixth sermon type in the clarification process uses an incident in the Bible such as a miracle and seeks to show how each

part of the incident contributes toward the unfolding of the purpose behind the incident. This purpose behind the incident
should be the timeless truth which it emphasizes. We can use
John 9:1-41 as a basis for demonstrating this sermon type. The
subject for such a sermon might read: "How God Works." The
theme could be "Component parts of the incident of the healing
of the man born blind as recorded in John 9:1-41 as these clarify
how God works." The proposition might read: "The incident of
the healing of the man born blind as recorded in John 9:1-41
helps to clarify how God works." The transitional sentence
might read: "An analysis of the incident of the healing of the
man born blind in John 9:1-41 into its component parts will
show how one segment of the account of the incident throws
light upon the subject of how God works."

### CLARIFYING THE IDENTITY OF GROUP MEMBERS

Sermon type number seven aims at clarifying the identity of the
individuals or groups included within a plural or collective personal noun or pronoun. The subject of such a sermon might be
"Tithing." The theme: "Church members and tithing." The
proposition: "Church members should practice tithing." The
transitional sentence: "The following individuals within the
church membership should practice tithing." The key word for
this sermon which will characterize the main point is the plural
noun "individuals." This sermon will proceed in its main points
to specify the individuals within the church membership who
should practice tithing. The first main point might read: "The
pastor should practice tithing." A sample sermon outline based
upon Colossians 3:18-4:1 is located near the end of this chapter.

These seven types of sermons which we have just discussed
have been formulated with the basic purpose in mind of imparting information. This information, however, has been imparted in
order that indirect persuasion may be brought upon the listeners.
It is hoped that when the listeners to the message understand,
they will then be prompted to respond by belief and practice.

Ian MacPherson quotes Boreham as saying, "I have never entered a pulpit . . . without feeling that, if only the people can
catch a vision of the Saviour, they would have no alternative but
to lay their devotion at His feet."[7]

## SAMPLE SERMON OUTLINE 1

PREACHING PORTION: Hebrews 12:1-17

SERMONIC PROCESS: Clar., Type 1

SUBJECT: Living the Christian Life

THEME: Comparisons between living the Christian life and running a race.

### The Race of Life

INTRODUCTION

*Approach Sentence:* Many who run in a race never win.

*Outlined Portion*

1.
2.

*Explanation*

1.
2.

PROPOSITION: Living the Christian life is like running a race.

TRANSITIONAL SENTENCE: The following comparisons between living the Christian life and running a race will help to clarify how we ought to live.

I. *Just as it is wise to avoid hindrances when one is running a race, so it is wise to avoid hindrances when one is living a Christian life.* Hebrews 12:1b—"Let us lay aside every weight, and the sin which doth so easily beset us."

1.
2.

(Illustration)

II. *Just as it is wise to profit from the experiences of great athletes of the past when one is running a race, so it is wise to profit from the experiences of great Christians who have lived for Christ in the past.* Hebrews 11-12:1a—"Wherefore seeing we also are compassed about with so great a cloud of witnesses." (12:1a).

1.

(Illustration)

2.

III. *Just as it is wise to keep one's mind on the finish line when running a race, so it is wise to keep one's mind on his ultimate goal when living the Christian life.* Hebrews 12:2—"Looking unto Jesus the author and finisher of our faith."

    1.
    2.
    (Illustration)
    3.

  IV. *Just as it is wise to be willing to submit to the directions of the coach when one is running a race, so it is wise to submit to the directions of our Lord when living a Christian life.* Hebrews 12:5-11—"He disciplines us for our good" (v. 10*b*, NASB).
    1.
    (Illustration)
    2.

CONCLUSION: Therefore, we as Christians should—
    1.
    2.

## SAMPLE SERMON OUTLINE 2

PREACHING PORTION: Psalm 103
SERMONIC PROCESS: Clar., Type 2
SUBJECT: Forgiveness
THEME: Definitions of Forgiveness

### Forgiven

INTRODUCTION
    *Approach Sentence:* Many are willing to forgive but will not forget.
    *Outlined Portion*
        1.
        2.
    *Explanation*
        1.
        2.

PROPOSITION: God forgives sin.

TRANSITIONAL SENTENCE: A study of the definitions of the English Bible word "forgive" will help clarify what is involved in God's forgiving sin.
  I. *The English Bible word* forgive *in Psalm 78:38 is the word* kophar *meaning "to cover."* "But he, being full of compassion forgave their iniquity."

  1.
  2.
  (Illustration)
  3.

 II. *The English Bible word* forgive *in Psalm 25:18 is the Hebrew word* nasa *meaning "to lift up or away."* "Look upon mine affliction and my pain; and forgive all my sins."
  1.
  2.
  (Illustration)
  3.

III. *The English Bible word* forgive *in Luke 7:43 is the Greek word* charizomai *meaning "to cancel a debt."* "I suppose that he, to whom he forgave most."
  1.
  (Illustration)
  2.
  3.

 IV. *The English Bible word* forgive *in Psalm 103:3 is the Hebrew word* salach *meaning "to send away."* "Who forgiveth all thine iniquities."
  (Illustration)
  1.
  2.

CONCLUSION: Therefore, we should—
  1.
  2.

## SAMPLE SERMON OUTLINE 3

PREACHING PORTION: Jonah 1
SERMONIC PROCESS: Clar., Type 3
SUBJECT: The Sovereignty of God
THEME: Evidences of the Sovereignty of God

### Who Is in Charge?

INTRODUCTION
  *Approach Sentence:*

*Outlined Portion*
    1.
    2.
*Explanation*
    1.
    2.

PROPOSITION: God is sovereign.

TRANSITIONAL SENTENCE: A study of the evidences of God's sovereignty will help to clarify the practical value of the doctrinal truth.

    I. *The doctrinal teaching that God is sovereign is evidenced in His designation of His workers.* Jonah 1:1—"Now the word of the LORD came unto Jonah."

      1.
      (Illustration)
      2.

    II. *The doctrinal teaching that God is sovereign is evidenced in His direction of His workers.* Jonah 1:2—"Arise, go to Ninevah."

      1.
      2.
      (Illustration)

    III. *The doctrinal teaching that God is sovereign is evidenced in His discipline of His workers.* Jonah 1:3-17—"But the LORD sent out a great wind into the sea" (v. 4).

      1.
      2.
      (Illustration)

CONCLUSION: Therefore, we should—

    1.
    2.

## SAMPLE SERMON OUTLINE 4

PREACHING PORTION: Numbers 32:6-32

SERMONIC PROCESS: Clar., Type 4

SUBJECT: The certainty of sin's discovery

THEME: Illustrations of the principle that you can be certain that sin will be discovered as set forth in the verse, "Be sure your sin will find you out." (Num 32:23)

## The Certainty of Discovery

INTRODUCTION

*Approach Sentence:* Are there many certainties?

*Outlined Portion*

   1.
   2.

*Explanation*

   1.
   2.

PROPOSITION: It is certain that sin will be discovered.

TRANSITIONAL SENTENCE: Illustrations of the principle that it is certain that sin will be discovered as set forth in Numbers 32:23, "Be sure your sin will find you out," will help to impress this truth upon us.

   I. *The principle that you can be certain that sin will be discovered as set forth in Numbers 32:23, "Be sure your sins will find you out," is illustrated in the experience of David and his sin against Bathsheba in 2 Samuel 11.*

   (Illustration)

   1.
   2.

   II. *The principle that you can be certain that sin will be discovered as set forth in Numbers 32:23, "Be sure your sin will find you out," is illustrated in the experience of Achan when he hid the spoil of battle in Joshua 7.*

   1.
   2.

   (Illustration)

   III. *The principle that you can be certain that sin will be discovered as set forth in Numbers 32:23, "Be sure your sin will find you out," is illustrated in the experience of Ananias and Sapphira when they lied to God in Acts 5.*

   1.
   2.

CONCLUSION: Therefore, we as Christians should—

   1.
   2.

## SAMPLE SERMON OUTLINE 5

PREACHING PORTION: Psalm 46:1-11

SERMONIC PROCESS: Clar., Type 5

SUBJECT: God's provision for us

THEME: Implications of the verse, "God is our refuge and strength, a very present help in trouble" as these help us understand God's provision for us

### God Provides

INTRODUCTION

*Approach Sentence:* What provisions do you have in readiness for an emergency?

*Outlined Portion*

    1.
    2.

*Explanation*

    1.
    2.

PROPOSITION: "God is our refuge and strength, a very present help in trouble" can help us understand God's provision for us.

TRANSITIONAL SENTENCE: The implications drawn from the words and phrases of this verse of Scripture can help us understand God's provision for us.

  I. *The verse contains the implication that this truth is centered in a person, "God."*

    1.
    2.
    (Illustration)

  II. *The verse contains the implication that our refuge is one for all times of tribulation, "very present."*

    1.
    2.

  III. *The verse contains the implication that our refuge is one which can be easily found, "very present."*

    1.
    (Illustration)
    2.

IV. *The verse contains the implication that our refuge consists of superlative protection, "help in trouble."*
(Illustration)

   1.

   2.

CONCLUSION: Therefore, we as Christians should—

   1.

   2.

## SAMPLE SERMON OUTLINE 6

PREACHING PORTION: John 9:1-41

SERMONIC PROCESS: Clar., Type 6

SUBJECT: How God Works

THEME: Component parts of the incident of the healing of the man born blind as recorded in John 9:1-41 as these clarify how God works.

### This Is How God Works

INTRODUCTION

*Approach Sentence:* We can learn about an individual by watching him work.

*Outlined Portion*

   1.

   2.

*Explanation*

   1.

   2.

PROPOSITION: The incident of the healing of the man born blind recorded in John 9:1-41 helps to clarify how God works.

TRANSITIONAL SENTENCE: An analysis of the incident of the healing of the man born blind as recorded in John 9:1-41 in its component parts will help to clarify how God works.

   I. *The description of the individual healed of his blindness as given in John 9:1-6 shows us that Christ works by grace.*

      1.

      2.

      (Illustration)

II. *The account of the cure applied to the man born blind as given in John 9:7-15 shows us that Christ works, providing man obeys.*
1.
2.

III. *The consequences resulting from the healing of the man born blind as given in John 9:16-41 shows us that Christ works in order that individuals might be brought into fellowship with Him.*
1.
(Illustration)
2.

CONCLUSION: Therefore, we as Christians should—
1.
2.

## SAMPLE SERMON OUTLINE 7

PREACHING PORTION: Colossians 3:18-4:1
SERMONIC PROCESS: Clar., Type 7
SUBJECT: The Christian family living to please the Lord
THEME: Living to Please the Lord

Pleasing the Lord as a Family

INTRODUCTION
*Approach Sentence:* The American family is in trouble.
*Outlined Portion*
1.
2.
*Explanation*
1.
2.

PROPOSITION: The Christian family should live to please the Lord.

TRANSITIONAL SENTENCE: Individuals within the Christian family should live to please the Lord.

MAIN DIVISIONS:
I. *The wife should submit herself to her own husband.* Colossians 3:18—"Wives, submit yourselves unto your own husbands, as it is fit in the Lord."

1.
2.
(Illustration)
3. Application

II. *The husband should love his wife.* Colossians 3:19—"Husbands love your wives."

   1.
   2.
   3. Application
   (Illustration)

III. *The husband (father) should encourage his children.* Colossians 3:21—"Fathers, provoke not your children to anger."

   1.
   (Illustration)
   2. Application

IV. *The children should obey their parents.* Colossians 3:20—"Children, obey your parents in all things: for this is well pleasing unto the Lord."

   1.
   (Illustration)
   2. Application

V. *The family servants should obey their employers.* Colossians 3:22 —"Servants, obey in all things your masters according to the flesh."

   (Illustration)
   1.
   2. Application

CONCLUSION: Therefore, we as family members should live to please the Lord.

1. "Whatsoever ye do, do it heartily as to the Lord, and not unto men." (3:23).
2. The Lord will reward our faithfulness (3:24).
3. If we do not live for the Lord, we shall receive for the wrong which we do since we have a Master in heaven (3:25, 4:1).

## Reading List

Baxter, Batsell Barrett. *The Heart of the Yale Lectures.* New York: Macmillan, 1950.

Braga, James. *How to Prepare Bible Messages.* Portland, Oreg.: Multnomah, 1969.

Brown, H. C., Jr.; Clinard, H. Gordon; and Northcutt, Jesse J. *Steps to the Sermon.* Nashville: Broadman, 1963.

Davis, H. G. *Design in Preaching.* Philadelphia: Muhlenberg, 1958.

Faw, Chalmer. *A Guide to Biblical Preaching.* Nashville: Broadman, 1962.

Garvie, Alfred Ernest. *The Christian Preacher.* New York: Scribner, 1921.

Koller, Charles W. *Expository Preaching Without Notes.* Grand Rapids: Baker, 1962.

Macleod, Donald. *Here is My Method.* Westwood, N.J.: Revell, 1952.

Miller, Donald G. *The Way to Biblical Preaching.* Nashville: Abingdon, 1957.

Perry, Lloyd M. *Biblical Sermon Guide.* Grand Rapids: Baker, 1970.

——————. *A Manual for Biblical Preaching.* Grand Rapids: Baker, 1965.

Phelps, Austin. *The Theory of Preaching.* London: Dickenson, 1882.

Roddy, Clarence Stonelynn, ed. *We Prepare and Preach.* Chicago: Moody, 1959.

Sangster, W. E.: *The Craft of the Sermon.* Philadelphia: Westminster, 1936.

Smithson, R. J. *My Way of Preaching.* London: Pickering, 1965.

Stevenson, Dwight E. *In the Biblical Preacher's Workshop.* Nashville: Abingdon, 1967.

Stewart, James S. *Heralds of God.* London: Hodder & Stoughton, 1946.

Whitesell, Faris D., and Perry, Lloyd M. *Variety in Your Preaching.* Westwood, N.J.: Revell, 1954.

# 4

## Biblical Preaching
## and Sermon Variation

"THE SECRET OF SPURGEON'S POWER was that he believed in the Bible from cover to cover. Spurgeon preached from the whole Bible. Wisely, he varied the sermon plans from week to week so that no listener could complain that the sermons sounded alike. Like his Master, Spurgeon cultivated what he called the 'surprise power.' "[1] This chapter is designed to help the preacher develop the "surprise power" in his own preaching.

The material in this discussion is divided into three major segments. We will first explore the methods which have been used in the past to classify conventional sermons. We will then suggest a method of classification of sermons which will expose the homiletician to some newer types of messages.* The third segment of the chapter will discuss cooperative preaching which is referred to by some as dialogical preaching. As we proceed with these three sections, we are beginning with tradition, expanding the traditional types of messages into newer types of sermons, and finally dealing with that which may be the latest star on the homiletical horizon—namely, the layman sharing with the clergy in the proclamation of the Word. We are not encouraging the preacher to change his basic message from the standpoint of content. We are encouraging him to change his method of construction and presentation.

*This material is amplified in section 3 of the book *Biblical Sermon Guide*, published by Baker Book in 1970.

## How Can We Classify Sermons?

How can we classify sermons? In recent years sermons have been classified from the standpoint of the manner of handling the text into *topical, textual, inferential* and *expository.*

Having noted this first method of classifying sermons and having elaborated upon it in the first chapter, we pass to a second possible classification method: mode of delivery. Within this we might include the *manuscript sermon.* Some prefer to read their sermons to the congregation, thus insuring accuracy of statements and logic. This method also helps the preacher stay within time limits. Such a sermon hampers gestures, however, and the manuscript produces a barrier between the speaker and his audience. If one desires to read the manuscript, care should be taken in its preparation. He should visualize his anticipated audience while writing. A complete outline should be formulated first, and then the manuscript written on the basis of the extensive outline. It is necessary to give careful consideration to the ideas rather than merely the words in presentation. Training should be obtained by the preacher in oral interpretation of literature. Manuscript preaching should be encouraged for such special occasions as preaching on the radio. In preparing the manscript, the preacher should "preach" the sermon into a recording device and have the secretary type the message from the tape. This will provide assistance in getting the sermon into oral style.

Next, there is the *memorized sermon.* The memorization of the manuscript for a presentation may be followed when there is a formal occasion, and when the accuracy of statement is a prime requisite. Such a method, however, places a heavy burden on the memory and tends to hamper naturalness in delivery. Only a few have memories adequate for such sermon presentation.

The *extemporaneous type* of delivery is the natural method and is convenient to use. The speaker is permitted to focus his whole attention on his audience, the message, and the techniques of voice and gesture. Good extemporaneous speaking is not easy. The speaker must practice constantly in order to develop exactness, correctness, and a good vocabulary. This method is dangerous for preachers who have more language than thought. The extemporaneous sermon may be delivered with notes. If this is the case, the preacher should make certain that the notes are written in clear form, condensed, and securely located on the pulpit. He should aim at never having to turn a page of notes within the pulpit. All the notes for the entire sermon should be on one side of a sheet of paper. The extemporaneous sermon may be delivered without notes. This is the ideal. In order to do this the preacher will have to give careful attention to the preparation of his outline. He must make certain that his outline is logical, simple, and clear. A good outline is one of the most important requirements if one is to preach without notes. The speaker must also be rested physically and mentally in order that he may concentrate on that which he desires to say. Preaching without notes gives him a freedom that no other method of delivery can offer him.

The third method for classifying sermons might be by occasion of delivery. In such a case there are two basic divisions within this classification—the ordinary or regular Sunday service sermon, and sermons delivered on special occasions. Virtually all of the sermons recorded in the Bible were special occasion messages. A seminary should face its responsibility at this point and provide the students with some assistance in meeting the challenge of preaching on a special occasion. An effective biblical message presented at a special occasion can be used by the Spirit of God in mighty ways. The seminary should also acquaint the student preacher with the major emphases of the Christian year.

Another method of sermon classification might be in terms of the emphasis or purpose of the sermon. A number of homiletics writers would classify sermons in this category under such headings as evangelistic, doctrinal, ethical, supportive, devotional, and actional.

There is a method of classifying sermons according to the method of treating the text. Austin Phelps says that this is the most important method of classification.[2] Four leading types might be noted here: (1) The *explanatory,* which involves the process of explaining what the thing it; (2) the *illustrative,* which is a descriptive discourse of a historical or biographical nature which makes truth lustrous; (3) the *argumentative,* the chief object of which is to prove a point; and (4) the *persuasive,* which includes an urgency for present action.

A sixth method for sermon classification might be in terms of the amount of biblical material within the text. Some homileticians refer to the *word-study sermon,* the *paragraph sermon,* the *chapter sermon,* and *Bible-book sermon* as being within this classification. Richard Waugh points out some of the preaching possibilities in just one word, such as the word "departure" in 2 Timothy 4:6, "The time of my departure is at hand":

1. It was a Seaman's Word, used for the "unloosing" of a ship from its anchorage:
2. It was a Ploughman's Term, denoting the "unyoking" of a weary team of horses after a toilsome day;
3. It was a Traveler's Expression, suggesting the "striking of a tent," preparatory to setting off on a march:
4. It was a Philosopher's Term, signifying the "solution of a problem."[3]

A seventh method of classification might be the special emphasis of the biblical material. There are at least two outstanding emphases which might be noted under this classification. First, is that of the *biographical emphasis.* Bible characters, both memorable and obscure, fit into the portrayal of God's relation to man and man's response to God's Word and God's will. Biographical sermons are interesting and useful. In doing biographical preaching one may base a sermon upon a *virtue* or *trait* to be emulated by Christians, an *event* or *series of events* in a character's life, the *inner life of the individual,* the *resolution of a conflict* within a life, or a *fault of a Bible character.*

The sermonizer should bear in mind the fact that he is interested in the production of character and in the regulation of conduct. In attempting to collect material for a biographical sermon, it is recommended that the sermonizer purchase two inexpensive Bibles, and cut out all the references to the particular Bible character on whom he desires to preach. He should then arrange these references in chronological order. This will mean that he will have formulated a Bible account covering all of the references to the experience of this character within Scripture. From this newly formulated collection of material he will then proceed to get his subject, theme, and sermon development. The sermonizer must beware of using these verses apart from the context in which they were originally located.

A sermonizer may find it helpful to answer the following questions regarding the particular Bible character which he is studying. The answers to the relevant questions should be noted in written form so that they may be used in connection with this particular sermon and also become a part of a file of information on Bible characters for future reference. The following questions might be asked and answered:

1. What sort of person was this?
2. What made him this sort of person?
3. What resulted from his being this sort of person?
4. What were the causes, preventatives, and cures of his weaknesses?
5. What were the secrets of his virtues?
6. How would you outline the character's life chronologically?
7. What is the meaning of the individual's name?
8. What is the ancestral background of the individual?
9. What significant religious and secular crises occured in his life?
10. What advantages for personal development were enjoyed by this individual?
11. What traits of character were manifest?
12. What important friends did this character have?
13. What important influence did this individual exert?
14. What failures and faults occured in this character's life?
15. What important contributions were made by this individual?
16. What one main lesson can be found within this life which is of special value to you?
17. What was the influence of the locality from the standpoint of geography, history, and culture upon this individual?
18. If this individual were in our present society, what would be his occupational or professional status?
19. What was this individual's relationship to God?
20. How can the gospel message be evidenced through this character?
21. How does this Bible character relate to the lives of the people who will be listening to this sermon?

22. With what enemies did he have to contend?
23. What motives were evidenced in the building of his life?

The sermonizer may also find it helpful to read Montgomery's treatment of biographical sermons in his book, *Preparing Preachers to Preach.*

The second special emphasis is that of emphasis upon *historical material.* Our primary interest in this regard is not history, but God in history. The preacher must make himself familiar with the country, people, customs, times, and other circumstances of the passage on which he intends to preach. This chosen passage must possess a basic unity. To get a lesson from a historical passage there must be a far sweep of the mind both broad and deep. Historical sermons stand in a class by themselves. They exemplify and enforce ethical principles from scriptural history and from the great characters depicted in its pages. In this type of sermonizing the preacher should concentrate on the passage until it has yielded up its inner secret, and upon the spirit of the passage, its emotional tone, until it has saturated the mind of the sermonizer.

The task of the preacher is two-fold in every sermon—to give knowledge and to produce faith. This type of sermon seeks to transform history into precept. As the preacher seeks to collect material regarding a historical passage in preparation for preaching, he may find it helpful to answer the following questions:

1. Why was this passage included in Scripture in the first place?
2. What does God seem to be saying to the people of our day through the events in this passage?
3. How could we outline the chronological unfolding of this entire passage?
4. What are the time limitations of this segment of Bible history and what other events were taking place at about this same period of time?
5. What do you know about the people who were involved in this segment of history?
6. What have you learned about the nature and actions of God as a result of studying this segment of Bible history?
7. How would you outline this portion of history?

8. Are there familiar verses within this segment which you've memorized or heard quoted through the years?
9. Is there a command, promise, or lesson which seems to summarize the practical preaching of the passage?
10. Are there words or phrases which are repeated several times throughout the passage?

Up to this point we have considered some seven methods for classifying sermons; there are still several others which might be added to this list. We note, therefore, that when someone asks, "What type of sermon is this?" it is difficult to know the type of answer which one should give.

## What are Some Ways to Gain Sermonic Variety?

It is our feeling that a more constructive approach to obtaining variety than merely noting the seven types of classification already cited, would be the *five-fold approach* which we outline in the following section.

### Sermon structure

First of all, variety may be gained by using different sermon structures. In the book, *Biblical Sermon Guide,* twenty-four different sermon structures are listed.[4] Some have two or three different names according to the label attached by particular authors. Some of these twenty-four structures are more helpful than others. One of the more common ones in use is the *adverbial or interrogative.* This sermon structure involves the division of the subject of the text by the application of several interrogative words. Such words as *who, what, why, where,* and *how* are often used. In using the subject "Prayer," the main divisions for such a sermon might be (1) What is prayer? (2) Who should pray? and (3) Why should we pray? This type of sermon is helpful in surveying and introducing a subject but has the drawback of being too broad and not deep enough.

The *couplet sermon* involves a sermon structure composed of two related parts. The first consists of an exhortation, and the second is the promise or practice drawn out of that exhortation. The two main divisions of the sermon should ideally come from the two parts of the text on which the preacher is preaching. Example: Malachi 3:10, "Bring ye all the tithes into the store-house, that there may be meat in mine house, and prove me now herewith, saith the LORD of hosts, if I will not open you the windows of heaven, and pour you out a blessing, that there shall not be room enough to receive it."

The *facet* or *jewel sermon* is one which takes a simple idea and then shows by relationships and applications the relevance of this idea to experience. The faceting process may involve emphases of origins, consequences, implications, or concrete instances.

The *Hegelian sermon* structure has three main divisions. The first states the thesis. The second states its opposite or the anti-thesis. And the third states the synthesis or the truth which emerges from the conflict of points one and two. Harold J. Ockenga has said that this is his favorite sermon structure.

The *inferential sermon* has also been known as the *deductive* or *implicational sermon*. This is one in which the text is the subject and the discussion consists of a series of inferences drawn directly from that text.

The *ladder, telescopic* or *pyramid sermon* has a structure in which each main division grows out of or builds upon the preceding point. Each point carries the subject out a little farther like the unfolding of a telescope or the lengthening of a ladder.

In the *objections answered sermon* we would have a structure arranged to answer the objections which the listener might have in mind as he hears the message. These are the objections which may keep him from accepting the truth of the sermon or from performing the activity advocated. Each objection would be listed as a main point of the message, and the amplification of that main point would include the answering of the objection.

The *propositional sermon* has a structure in which the proposition clearly states the subject of the sermon and the task which the sermon proposes to accomplish.

The *question sermon* is one in which each main point of the message is stated in the form of a question. The amplification of each point involves the answering of that question.

Stidger made the *symphonic sermon* famous. The sermon is

built around the couplet, which is repeated throughout the sermon until it is locked in the memory of the hearers. Example: Who is going to guard the Coast Guard while the Coast Guard is guarding the coast?

The *textual sermon* finds the basis for its structure within the text. The text is divided, and the main divisions of the sermon are suggested by words and phrases within the text itself. Example: 2 Chronicles 7:14, "If my people, which are called by my name, shall humble themselves, and pray, and seek my face, and turn from their wicked ways; then will I hear from heaven, and will forgive their sin, and will heal their land."

Some of the additional identifications for sermons according to structure might include:

| | |
|---|---|
| the analytical sermon | Roman Candle sermon |
| the chase technique sermon | sky-rocket sermon |
| guessing game sermon | suppositional sermon |
| devotional sermon | surprise package sermon |
| dramatic continuity sermon | synthetical sermon |
| inductive sermon | natural sermon |
| pictorial sermon | comprehensive sermon |
| practical sermon | the twin-point sermon |

All of these sermon structures have been referred to in one or more homiletic books. The books and authors noting these types of sermons are listed in the *Biblical Sermon Guide*.[5]

### BIBLICAL SUBJECT MATTER

Variety in one's preaching can also be gained by using different biblical subject matter. The sermonizer will find it profitable to give consideration to preaching on some of these items found in the Scriptures:

| | |
|---|---|
| admonitions | benedictions |
| antithetical segments | births |
| apocalyptic passages | character sketches |
| apostasies | churches |
| battles | commandments |
| beatitudes | contributions of Bible characters |

conversations
conversions
covenants
crises
doctrinal portions
dramatic portions
epitaphs
family life experiences
figures of speech
fools
funerals
geographical locations
historical material and
   journeys
historical turning points
hymns or songs of the Bible
interesting incidents
judgments
life principles of Bible
   characters
marriages of the Bible

men and women of prayer
miracles
mountains
names of God
night scenes
parables
paradoxes
periods of Bible history
poetical portions
prayers
prophetic passages
questions
revivals
romances
sermons
spies
theophanies
trees
trials of great persons
types and visions

This will give the sermonizer fifty-one different types of biblical content to include as bases for sermonizing.

PORTIONS OF THE BIBLE

The preacher may add variety to his preaching by using different sized portions of the Bible. He may want to preach on a book of the Bible within one sermon. For example, he may want to preach on the book of Ruth under the theme, "Triumphant Faith," or the book of Esther under the theme, "The Protection of Providence," or the book of James under the theme, "Practical Christianity." He might also write a sermon on a chapter of the Bible. Some suggestions might include:

Psalm 19, "How God Speaks."
Isaiah 53, "The Gospel According to Isaiah."
Romans 8, "More than Conquerors."
Hebrews 11, "Faith in Action."

Beyond the book or chapter he might preach upon a paragraph of the Bible:

> Joshua 1:1-9, "Secrets of Success."
> Mark 5:1-20, "When Jesus Comes."
> 2 Timothy 4:6-8, "The Satisfaction of a Godly Life."
> Philippians 4:4-7, "A Prescription for Peace."

He might want to preach on a verse of the Bible, such as Luke 9:33, including "The Demands of Discipleship." He might finally want to construct a sermon on a key word or key phrase in the Bible. The word *straightway* in the gospel of Mark, which occurs forty-two times, might suggest the basis for a sermon, or the word *better* which is used some eleven times in the book of Hebrews.

## STARTING SERMON IDEA

The fourth means of gaining variety in one's sermonizing is to use a starting sermon idea from an extrabiblical source. Although the idea for such a sermon has its genesis outside the actual Scripture, its truth must correspond to biblical truth. Unless the idea and its development can be supported from the Scripture, it should not be used. These types of sermons will be strengthened by the use of visual aids in their presentation. Because of the uniqueness of their content, they'll prove helpful in meeting the challenges offered by special occasions. The preacher must be careful lest he become so involved with the unique source of his preaching idea that he forget that his primary task is to use this only as a vehicle for presenting the biblical truth in a more effective manner.

Such starting sermon ideas might be found in the following:

> Christian classics
>> John Bunyan's *Pilgrims Progress*
>> Brother Laurence's *Practicing the Presence of God*
> church history
> denominational distinctives
> the account of the life of a great Christian
>> David Brainard (John 7:37-38)

a great hymn of the church
    Luther's "A Mighty Fortress is Our God"
a famous painting
    "Christ Before Pilate"
a great poem
    "The Touch of the Master's Hand"
a famous quotation or popular slogan
an object or a hobby
    stamp collecting

The basis for each main point within such a sermon will be obtained from the extrabiblical source, but this basis will be shown to be in accord with the general teaching and emphasis of Scripture. The sermonizer will thus be using this extrabiblical starting point as a vehicle for enforcing and clarifying a message of biblical truth.

PURPOSE OF THE SERMON

Homiletical writers encourage the sermonizer to obtain variety in his preaching by placing special emphasis on the purpose of the sermon. The following types of sermons might be catalogued in terms of the purpose emphasized:

the apologetic sermon
the argumentative sermon
the classification or categorizing sermon
the commentary sermon
the corrective or rebuttal sermon
the doctrinal or theological sermon
the ethical sermon which is one form of a
    life-situation or problem sermon
the evangelistic or soul-winning sermon
the expansive or observational sermon
the experiential sermon
the expository sermon
the narrative sermon
the orientation sermon
the persuasive sermon

the social sermon
the spiritualizing sermon

The final type—the *topical, thematic,* or *selective sermon*—is a sermon which is occupied with one subject. The subject may be drawn from a text, but it is discussed independently of that text. In this type of sermon the purpose is to partition the subject according to its inherent nature.

It is not a matter of primary importance that the sermonizer be able to give a clear identifying label to each type of sermon which he uses. It is important that the sermon be *biblical in content, logical in organization, practical in application, and varied in structure and presentation.*

## WHAT CONTRIBUTION DOES DIALOGICAL PREACHING MAKE TO SERMON VARIATION

One of the most significant trends in modern preaching is the challenging of the conventional sermon which has been mono-logical in presentation and the growing emphasis and demand for dialogical preaching. The conventional sermon makes preach-ing the exclusive responsibility of the preacher and tends to draw some unwarranted lines of distinction between the preacher and the laymen. This type of monological performance gives no op-portunity for feedback.

This type of presentation has some weaknesses in terms of communication. One research project concludes that "Mass communication can be effective in producing a shift on un-familiar, lightly felt, peripheral issues—those that do not matter much to the audience. . . . On the others, it is effective in reinforcing opinions but only infrequently changes them."[6] If the conclusions of this research are valid, then the conven-tional sermon involving mass communication will tend to strengthen the convictions already held by the listeners, but will not prove very successful in changing those deeply rooted con-victions and ingrained behavior patterns.

It is not wise for the preacher to ignore the value to be gained by participative relationships in the preaching process. One of the purposes of a sermon is to instruct the listener. Educational theory emphasizes the need for a sharing between the teacher and the students or, in our context, between the preacher and his congregation.

It is charged that the modern preacher uses theological jargon which irritates the laymen largely because he doesn't understand it. The language is often the technical language of the theologian. Another charge is that of irrelevance. Reuel Howe in his article in *Pastoral Psychology* entitled, "The Recovery of Dialogue in Preaching," quotes a layman as saying that he was sick and tired of being talked to by his preacher as if he were a "Corinthian." The charge of formalism has been leveled against the conventional sermon whereas modern living tends toward informality. It stresses the need for an emphasis upon the individual. The monological sermon is often quite impersonal and general. It is the feeling of a number that conventional preaching is characterized by cowardice. Harvey Cox, says, "Our preaching today is powerless because it does not confront people with the new reality which has occurred and because the summons is issued in general rather than in specific terms."[7]

This cowardice in preaching may not only be evidenced in presenting generalities without specifics but also in failing to stand by one's convictions.

This is a day of rapid change. Such change is challenging, upsetting, and often disturbing. As the preacher seeks to recognize and cope with these changes, new ways of doing things may have to be developed. It will take some stalwart resolve to institute changes which he is convinced are needed for enhancing the presentation of the gospel.

Many feel that traditionalism hampers the effectiveness of present-day preaching. It is the feeling of some that our modern method of conventional preaching is guilty of overcommunication. Clyde Reid states,

> One of the great dilemmas in the present pattern of the church life is the sheer volume of information we present to our congregations. Week after week, we present them with additional ideas, concepts, duties, and responsibilities, with no opportunity to talk back, to wrestle with those ideas, to absorb and integrate the content before we dump some more. It is little wonder that the seed

lies on top of the ground and does not put down roots in the lives of the listeners.[8]

The conventional sermon conceives of communication as a one way process. This originates in a transmission theory of education wherein truth transfer is automatic. Both the preacher and his people suffer when such a process is exclusively employed. The preacher feels threatened by advances being made in the field of secular mass communication media. He feels frustrated since he feels that he is not getting through to his people in a way that encourages a change in their living. He realizes that he must try to escape the fallacy of the elocutionists who felt that giving a good performance was an end in itself. This one-way process of communication encourages the layman to become dependent and silent. He is thus indirectly encouraged to become critical. He draws the implication that he is not competent to become involved. An attitude of hostility may even develop since there is a natural tendency to resent authoritarianism.

What do we mean by dialogue?

Reuel Howe has written some of the most definitive material on dialogue in relation to preaching.

> Dialogue is that address and response between persons in which there is a flow of meaning between them in spite of all the obstacles that normally would block the relationship. It is that interaction between persons in which one of them seeks to give himself as he is to the other . . . as the other is. This means that he will not attempt to impose his own truth and view on the other. Such is the relationship which characterizes dialogue and is the precondition to dialogical communication.[9]

Communication is not a one-way process, but is rather a complex, two-way relationship. The word "communication" is derived from the Latin *communis,* meaning "common." To communicate is to establish a "commonness" with the receiver. It involves the sharing of information, ideas and attitudes.

A study of the methods of communication of the Word of God in biblical times reveals that the method differed from the typical lecture-sermon of our present day. Preaching consisted of reading a passage of Scripture followed by clarification or exposition. In the service, any qualified person was permitted to speak, to argue, or to discuss.

Jesus preached few sermons patterned after our conventional sermons which are preached today. Of some 125 incidents recorded in the gospels wherein Jesus communicated with people, about 54 percent were initiated by the auditors. His communication was characterized by a conversation with questions and answers, objections, debate, agreement, and rejection.

The apostles also engaged in multilateral preaching. They disputed in the synagogues (Ac 17:17; 18:4) and "in reasoning daily" in the school of Tyrannus (Ac 19:9). From a study of the sermons of these men we gather that the auditors were free to interact with them. William Thompson writes:

> The first Christians, as you know were Jews. After their conversion to Christianity, they had no reason to change their basic pattern of worship—only their interpretation of the scriptures. Even the Gentile converts took over the rather informal synagogue worship in which the people sang songs, prayed, read scriptures and shared in interpreting them.

He then goes on to say,

> It did not occur to the very first Christians to delegate the responsibility for preaching or officiating in worship exclusively to one of their members. The entire church shared the responsibility.[10]

Not only does the Bible commend multilateral preaching, but our day seems to have a demand for it. In days past, the preacher was often the best educated man in the community, and the best qualified to speak on most issues. This has changed. Leslie Tizard writes: "Many a minister now has to recognise that there is probably somebody who knows more about every subject than he does with the possible exception of divinity—and some of us cannot even be sure of that!"[11]

Several years ago there was a growing sense of need for a cooperative type of preaching. Harry Emerson Fosdick, in an article entitled "What is the Matter with Preaching?" which appeared in *Harper's Magazine* back in 1928, wrote:

> When a man has got hold of a real difficulty in the life and thinking of his people and is trying to meet it, he finds himself not so

much dogmatically thinking for them as cooperatively thinking with them. His sermon is an endeavor to put himself in their places and help them think their way through.

He then proceeds to make reference to the type of preacher who plays Sir Oracle and says,

> Their method, however, has long since lost its influence over intelligent people, and the future does not belong to it. The future, I think, belongs to a type of sermon which can best be described as an adventure in cooperative thinking between the preacher and his congregation.[12]

In a thesis written as a partial fulfillment of the required work for a Master of Theology degree at Trinity Evangelical Divinity School, Wesley Pinkham made a correlation of possible methods for incorporating dialogical preaching into a church program. The suggestions were grouped in three categories—those which might be employed before the actual sermon was delivered, those which might be employed in connection with the actual delivery of the sermon, and finally those which might be carried out after the delivery of the sermon. These methods which can become a part of a multilateral ministry provide basic suggestions for developing a cooperative type of preaching ministry. Dialogical preaching should not be considered as a substitute for monological preaching, but should be used on occasion to supplement it.

I. *Before the actual delivery of the sermon:*

> The congregation can be encouraged to engage in preliminary private study in preparation for hearing the sermon by having the preacher make assignments for study based upon forthcoming preaching passages.

> Small groups can be formed for studying the scriptural portion which forms the basis for the sermon of the next Sunday.

> A sermon seminar can be held in which a pastor gives explanatory material regarding the context, exegetical comments on the contents, and items of concern based on the scriptural portion to be used as a base for the forthcoming sermon. Groups are then formed to reduce this material to principles. Implications are drawn and applications made.

The pastor circulates from group to group getting sermonic help for the sermon which he is to write and deliver.

A sermon board can be formed with eight representative members. The members rotate quarterly. The pastor meets with this sermon board weekly to discuss previously assigned preaching portions in light of the basic question: "What do I need to say to you from this portion of scripture?"

II. *During the actual delivery of the sermon:*

A one-man, one-voice dialogue can be employed. The pastor seeks to anticipate the questions which his people would ask if they were given an opportunity. His sermon consists of asking and answering these questions.

A dialogue sermon can be used in which two or more people give the sermon. One may speak from the pulpit and one from the congregation, or they may speak from separate pulpits. For instance, one speaker might present the message of God and the other present the counter message of Satan.

A discussion sermon can be used in which the members of the congregation interact verbally with the pastor and with each other. If this is used, adequate provision should be made for amplification in order that all may hear the discussion. The discussion sermon could be developed in accordance with the discussion method as set forth in the book *Discussion in Human Affairs,* by McBurney and Hance.

Lay preaching may be used. This in principle involves the congregation preaching to itself.

III. *After the actual delivery of the sermon:*

An after service forum may be held. This is sometimes held in place of an adult Sunday school class. Some churches hold such a forum after the evening service. At this time, the congregation discusses the content and applications of the preceeding sermon.

Some churches have tried a talk-back sermon. The pastor presents a message in the morning service and the congregation responds to it during the evening message time.

A feedback group or sermon seminar may be held without the pastor being present. This feedback group evaluates the message which the pastor presented. The following questions are some which might be posed:

1) What did this sermon actually say to you?
2) What difference if any do you think the message will make in your life?
3) In what ways did the pastor help or hinder in the presentation of his thoughts?

The discussion of these and other questions is taped in order that the pastor may listen to the recording at a later time.

One congregation has developed a midweek service in which a 20- or 30-minute service and message is provided in the sanctuary. The congregation and pastor then retire to the fellowship room for a refreshment time and discussion time. The benediction is not given until after the discussion.

Some churches have held dialogue luncheons. The leader makes a 15-minute presentation while the other attendants are eating. After the message there is a 30-minute discussion by the group.[13]

The change from the monological presentation to that of a co-operative approach involves a change of method but does not demand a change in the basic message. Thompson and Bennett deal with dialogue as a method of preaching rather than as a principle. They, therefore, regard it as an act within the context of public worship in which two or more persons engage in a verbal exchange as the sermon or message.[14] Irrespective of the method used, the message must have the contents of the Christian faith. Discussion of matters of sociology, economics, ethics, or politics should be secondary to the discussion of matters pertaining to the Christian faith.

The preacher should not be the leader of discussion groups which are held in connection with consideration of his message. If this were to be done then we would be maintaining the same dependance pattern which is fostered by the monological approach. If dialogue patterns are used which involve the congregation taking part in small groups, it is suggested that the same people be kept in a given group for a period of time.

Cooperative preaching or dialogical preaching will encourage the laymen in our churches to share their convictions and experiences with others. This type of presentation can be one in which feelings and concerns are shared and trust can emerge. Cooperative preaching even as conventional preaching must have as its basic purpose the proclamation of the good news of Jesus Christ. The presentation will be established upon a biblical foundation.

We have discussed many methods which may be employed in cooperative preaching. The naive may feel that, merely by employing one of the many methods outlined, he can thus become involved in effective cooperative preaching. There is more involved than merely adopting a method of presentation.

Preparing for cooperative preaching demands more time and work than preparing for conventional preaching. At this point, I disagree with Thompson and Bennett who feel that dialogical preaching takes far less preparation.[15] It takes more time to prepare the different methodology of delivery. It also takes more time to discover and arrange the content.

Dialogue depends upon discussion. The sermon must include material which is thought provoking and opens areas for discussion. Historical, geographical, and biographical facts do not normally stimulate discussion, but rather when presented tend to close discussion. Many conventional sermons emphasize facts of the past and merely provide spiritually flavored comments on events in the past.

Thompson and Bennett include an extensive discussion of dialogue in the chancel. In this type of preaching two or more persons converse between themselves in front of a congregation. The listeners in the congregation do not share verbally in just dialogue but do share psychologically as they agree or disagree with positions presented by the participants. This dialogue may be carried on between clergymen, clergy and laity, or clergy and youth. The subject matter may include matters of faith, inquiry into problems, or the sharing of opposing ideas which are held by friendly people. Some dialogical preaching takes the form of a type of dramatization. It is not play acting but rather the conveying a message through drama-related activities. In this country to some extent, but more especially in England, more attention is being paid to training the preacher in the dramatic arts. This change in training emphasis may be related to the new emphasis upon dialogical preaching.

There is also congregational dialogue which involves the congregation in worship by inviting spontaneous questions and responses. This is a form of feedback during the sermon rather than waiting until after the sermon. Feedback during or after the message demands that discussion stimulators be present.[16]

Discussion is stimulated when the preacher surveys the past in search of timeless truths. History does not repeat itself. Today is always different from yesterday. There are, however, certain timeless principles which run as threads through the cloth of time. Since God is changeless, it is profitable for the sermonizer to seek to discover what the scriptural account teaches about the changeless God. What is God like? How does God work? What is God doing? What is God trying to teach us? Profitable discussions can arise as the sermonizer together with his congregation seek to discover the teachings of the passage about God.

Discussion is stimulated as the sermonizer and his congregation seek to establish the original purpose behind the presentation of the passage of Scripture when it was first conveyed, and the relevance of that purpose to our present day. In some cases the purpose is clearly stated in scripture. In such cases there is nothing to discuss. There it is. In other cases, the purpose must be determined from the content or from outside sources. Discussion is stimulated by the search for purpose.

Discussion is stimulated as the sermonizer and his congregation seek for methods of applying timeless principles to present day living. Many conventional sermons are weak in the area of application. People in different occupations apply principles in different ways. To the doctor it means this, but to the schoolteacher it may mean something else. The sermonizer must strive to see life through the eyes of his listener and be prepared to show possible methods for the application of truth to life.

Discussion is stimulated as the sermonizer and his congregation survey the implications of scriptural segments and their timeless truths. The denotative or literal meaning of a word for instance can be discovered in the dictionary or lexicon. We look it up, read it, and there the matter closes. The connotation of a word involves the suggestive emotional content and significance of a word beyond its literal meaning. This type of meaning gives us something to discuss.

Discussion is stimulated as the sermonizer preaches sermons which help the congregation discover biblical answers for present day problems. These should be problems which are related to the living of the immediate congregation. Some have suggested that each sermon should be designed to solve some problem. Others have suggested that each sermon should be designed to answer a question. If such a procedure is followed, the sermonizer should make certain that the question which the sermon seeks to answer is a question which someone in the congregation is asking. Maybe we spend too much time trying to answer questions which no one is asking. The investigation sermonic process discussed in chapter 5 lends itself to cooperative preaching.

Doctrinal sermons would stimulate more discussion if they emphasized the practical applications of the doctrine to daily living. Many people have developed a dislike for doctrinal sermons. Some of this dislike has developed through an emphasis in the sermon upon the doctrine but not upon the duty evolving from it. The sermonizer has stressed the creed, but not the conduct related to that creed. Creedal discussions often move in the realm of the technical. This technical, theological terminology is not known by the average member of the congregation. The average member of the congregation would not be interested in becoming involved in such a discussion. The discussion might be more spiritually profitable by placing emphasis on biblical rather than systematic theology.

How can the sermonizer be sure that his sermon will stimulate discussion? He should know his people. A good salesman knows his prospect as well as his product. He should seek to know the problems of his people. He should write his sermon with his people in mind. The main points of the sermon should be formulated with wording of a timeless nature. As many of the subdivisions as possible should also be formulated in this way. The wording should be such that it will suggest expansion and application.

During the construction of the sermon, the sermonizer should be asking, "What will this mean to the listeners?" When the sermonizer constructs the sermon with this in mind, the receiver of the sermon will be encouraged to discover and apply sermonic truth to life.

If the preacher expects the people to find something in the sermon which will prompt discussion, then he should be able to write out a list of areas for discussion which have come to him during the process of preparation.

Preaching, whether it be conventional or cooperative, must have as its message the Word of God and this must be presented as a message from God who is speaking to His people. The aims of the preaching should be evangelization and edification. The preacher, with the help of the Spirit of God, must make clear the relevance of the message to the culture, sentiments, sympathies, and situation of the congregation. The message should be logical, scholarly, Bible-centered, heart-centered, and life-centered.

## Reading List

Cox, Harvey. *The Secular City*. New York: Macmillan, 1966.

Howe, Reuel L. *The Miracle of Dialogue*. New York: Seabury, 1963.

––––––. *Partners in Preaching*. New York: Seabury, 1967.

Jones, Ilion T. *Principles and Practices of Preaching*. New York: Abingdon, 1956.

Kraus, Hans-Joachin. *The Threat and the Power*. Richmond: John Knox, 1971.

Luccock, Halford E. *In the Minister's Workshop*. New York: Abingdon-Cokesbury, 1944.

Mark, Harry C. *Patterns for Preaching*. Grand Rapids: Zondervan, 1959.

Montgomery, R. Ames. *Preparing Preachers to Preach*. Grand Rapids: Zondervan, 1939.

Mullen, Thomas J. *The Dialogue Gap*. Nashville: Abingdon, 1969.

Phelps, Austin. *The Theory of Preaching*. New York: Scribner, 1894.

Randolph, David James. *The Renewal of Preaching*. Philadelphia: Fortress, 1969.

Reid, Clyde. *The Empty Pulpit*. New York: Harper & Row, 1967.

Stidger, William L. *Building Sermons with Symphonic Themes*. New York: Doran, 1926.

Tizard, J. Leslie. *Preaching: The Art of Communication*. London: Oxford, 1958.

# 5

# Biblical Preaching
## and Life-Situation Preaching

HOMILETICAL ORTHODOXY should combine the good news and the contemporary situation. We need more sermons which try to face the real problems of the people, help meet their difficulties, answer their questions, confirm their noblest faith, and interpret their experiences with sympathetic, wise understanding and cooperation.

Many feel that preaching should advance to territories from which Christianity has virtually been expelled in these recent years; such areas as politics, economics, industry, science, education, and art. It is true that the sovereignty of God extends not only over prayer and worship, but over all activities and institutions. The Christian preacher has an opportunity and a responsibility to set forth the Christian principles and point out where the existing social order is at variance with them. This means he will not only preach on personal problems, but upon community problems and national problems as well. The preacher will want to concentrate on the description of the cure as much as upon the diagnosis of the cause.

The prophetic responsibility which rests upon the preacher cannot be fulfilled until the preacher speaks to the needs of men in the pews in a way that can be understood and acted upon by them. I agree with W. M. MacGregor who states "It is indispensable for a preacher that he should know men, what they are and how they think and feel."[1] It was said of Philip Henry that he did not shoot the arrow of the Word over the heads of his audience in affected rhetoric, not under their feet by homely expression, but to their heart in close and lively application.[2]

There is a need for the preacher of today to proclaim the good news of the gospel in such a way that men will be drawn to God, to preach it in such a way that they will see its beauty and power, and to preach it in such a way that they will be able to put its truth into daily practice.

The preacher stands in the gap between the demands of God and the deepest needs of man. His task is to bring the two together. Ideally, the sermon should bring the great affirmations of faith and the great issues of life together like great electrodes in an arch light. They will be close enough together to enable the fires of kindling knowledge, hope, and strength to leap into being. Robert McCracken commented, "The pulpit is under obligation to urge Christians as citizens to come to grips with these evils [corruption, graft, juvenile and adult delinquency, drunkeness, gambling, bad houses and unfair labor practices] and subdue them."[3]

Leslie Tizard said, "Whoever will become a preacher must feel the needs of men until it becomes an oppression to his soul."[4] Jesse McNeil puts it this way, "The preacher-prophet today who concerns himself with the ethical and social relationships of organized community life as a spokesman for God stands in the best tradition of the true prophets of old and follows in the footsteps of his Lord and Master, Jesus Christ."[5]

The sermon dealing with a problem should aim to comfort men and women with the comfort whereby we are comforted by the Holy Spirit, thus imparting the comfort of God. It should show the joy of the Lord to troubled souls. A good sermon dealing with problems should tie biblical content to specific life problems:

> We might take for example Exodus 15:22-27 and consider the problem of facing life's disappointments. In Exodus 15, two million souls have been on their march from the land of bondage to the land of blessings for three days. They have been walking without water. The first of the three days probably had passed as novelty; but as the second and third days of waterless wanderings came, their singing

turns to sorrow. They had been minstrels before, but now they became murmurers. They had left the green fertility of the Nile and now faced the silence of the desert. As they trudged from the sea to Shur along the narrow strip of land about ten to fifteen miles wide, they came face to face with one of the many testings by God as He led them to the land of the plenty.

Word was passed back through their lines that water was just ahead. With parched throats and weary feet, they hastened their step. As the first in line knelt by the water and cupped it to his mouth there came a shout of anguish, "The water is bitter." What would you have done if you had been there? Or maybe we should ask, What do you do when your expectations are shattered and the water of life is found to be bitter?

Try to discover the purpose behind the disappointment. "There he made for them a statute and an ordinance, and there he proved them" (v. 25).

Try to recognize the real person behind the disappointment, not the most likely person at hand. "And the people murmured against Moses" (v. 24).

Try to employ God's process for overcoming the disappointment. Moses "cried unto the Lord" (v. 25).

Just beyond the bitter waters of Marah lay Elim where there were twelve wells of water and seventy palm trees. Beyond the bitterness, God knows the location of an oasis of refreshment.

We might check also Joshua 7:1-5 and note the situation of defeat. This should be surveyed with the aim of getting help as to how to diagnose our defeats. Defeat is a school in which truth always grows stronger. Defeat sometimes leads to despair; but, when it is faced in a wise fashion, profitable results can accrue.

The silent majority had marched around the great city of Jericho. Only trumpets broke the silence. On the seventh day they circled it seven times, and after thirteen trips the trumpets were blown and the walls fell. It seems as though God had them march long enough to realize that, when the victory would come, it would be all of God and not of men. The conquest of Canaan took seven years. There was only one defeat in the campaign, and thirty-six men were lost. This all happened at Ai. God wanted victory for His people, but His people brought defeat upon themselves.

The diagnosis of a defeat is not a simple matter. There is often the outward sin which becomes clear to all. Around this one sin, there are often those elements which set the stage for specific outward sin. Three were evidenced in this total incident—namely, overconfidence in oneself (7:3), failure to wait upon God (7:10), and disobedience to the commands of God (7:11).

### TERMS USED TO IDENTIFY SUCH PREACHING

This type of problem preaching has been referred to by different authors, each using distinctive terminology:

1. It has been referred to as *life-situation preaching*, by Halford Luccock in his book *The Minister's Workshop;* by Andrew Blackwood in his book *Preparation of Sermons;* by Gerald R. Jordan in his book *You Can Preach;* by Frank Caldwell in his book *Preaching Angles;* and by Charles Kemp in his book *Life-Situation Preaching.*
2. Caldwell referred to it as *problem-solving preaching,* as well.
3. James Cleland in his book *Preaching to be Understood,* calls it *bifocal preaching.*
4. George Gibson in his book *Planned Preaching,* refers to it as *personal problem preaching.*
5. David MacLennan and Henry Sloan Coffin called it *pastoral preaching.*
6. Edmond Linn in his book *Preaching as Counseling,* which is a summary of Harry Emerson Fosdick's homiletical method, refers to this type of preaching as *counseling preaching.*
7. Wayne Oates in the *Christian Pastor,* calls it *therapeutic preaching.*
8. Charles Jefferson in his two books *The Minister as a Prophet*

and *The Minister as a Shepherd,* refers to it as *preventive preaching.*

9. The term *ethical preaching* is given to it by James Hoppin in his book *The Office and Work of the Christian Ministry;* also by Lewis Brastow in his book *The Work of the Preacher.*

10. Robert J. McCracken published a book *The Making of the Sermon.* In that book he referred to it as *social preaching.*

We would agree with Walter R. Bowie that every sermon ought to be related to the needs of life[6] and with Charles Smith who says that the sermon should aim to reach people as human beings, to speak to their human situation, and lead them to see the glorious possibilities human beings can attain under God.[7]

TESTIMONY FROM THE HISTORY OF PREACHING

A study of the history of preaching reveals that preaching on problems has been employed by preachers for many years. F. R. Webber, in his work *A History of Preaching,* indicates that the friars in prereformation Scotland (16th Century) "were content to condemn the evils of their day: drunkenness, profanity, theft, immorality and cruelty."[8] Dargan indicates that similar preaching was done also in the fifteenth century. The Moderates, a liberal party in the Scottish church of the late seventeenth and eighteenth centuries employed what might be called life-situation preaching. Webber later points out that as this tendency kept recurring in the church, the emphasis upon sin and salvation would often be diminished. In the third volume of his work, Webber states:

> In many instances there is less doctrinal preaching, but rather is there an indication of stress upon the ethical and the practical. The American pulpit, which had always been influenced by Europe, is beginning to make a contribution of its own to the history of preaching, and an American style is in the process of development.[9]

Great issues in America made life-situation preachers out of many. The issues of slavery and prohibition were two such issues.

Webber goes on to state that "in our day it has become the fashion to discuss personality problems in the pulpit."[10] Ronald Sleeth in *Proclaiming the Word* also takes note of the shift toward life-situation preaching.[11]

### Testimony from Text and Tradebooks in Homiletics

A survey of sixty-eight American textbooks in homiletics, written by American-born teachers of homiletics between 1834 and 1954 indicated that the life-situation sermon per se was not referred to in these texts prior to 1944. It also pointed out the fact that the four outstanding books dealing with this type of preaching were *In the Minister's Workshop* by Luccock, *The Preparation of Sermons* by Blackwood, *You Can Preach* by Jordan, and *Preaching Angles* by Caldwell.[12]

### Preachers Noted for This Type of Preaching

If we were to make a list of some of the preachers who have been noted for preaching upon problems whether personal, community, or national, we might include such men as:

Albert W. Beaven (1882-1943), with his fireside sermons.

Henry Ward Beecher (1813-87), with his sermons against drinking, gambling, and slavery.

John Sutherland Bonnell (1892-    ), with his counseling through preaching.

Walter Russell Bowie (1882-    ), with his emphasis upon knowing his people personally.

Horace Bushnell (1802-76), with his emphasis upon pastoral work and counseling.

Jack Finegan (1908-    ), with his emphasis upon the problems faced by university students.

Harry Emerson Fosdick (1878-1969), with his emphasis upon the fact that every sermon should have as its main business the solving of some problem.

Arthur J. Gossip (1873-1954), noted for his study of his congregation. His sermons brought hope and cheer from the Scriptures.

Robert McCracken (1904-73), Harry Emerson Fosdick's successor
at the Riverside Church in New York.

Norman Vincent Peale (1898-    ), with his emphasis upon
the power of positive thinking as he seeks to meet the common
man's problems.

F. W. Robertson (1816-53), with his concern for the intellectual
and social problems of his day, thus arousing suspicion on the
part of his conservative Christian colleagues.

Leslie Weatherhead (1893-    ), with his emphasis upon the
correlation between psychology and religion.

Clarence S. Roddy, says, in regard to the life-situation sermon:
"The sermon grows out of a life situation known to the pastor.
It presents an existential problem which calls for a solution
from the Word of God. . . . It must always be kept in mind that
the solution is not found in the characters involved but in their
*God or Christ.*"[13]

A life-situation sermon might be built upon Isaiah 55:1-13,
where God speaks to His chosen people to assure them of His
continuing care and presence, even in the midst of their
chastisement.

> Let us look for example at Isaiah 55:1-13 and note God's
> provision for guaranteed satisfaction. The people to whom
> this chapter was first directed were displaced, disillusioned,
> disheartened, and despairing. They were going through
> life without hope. They had suffered hardships, heartaches,
> and hopelessness. This chapter with its invitation to come
> to God for satisfaction must have blessed their hearts like
> a cool breeze after a hot day. It was Clarence McCartney
> who referred to *come* as God's favorite word. He has invited
> folk to come to Him for safety, sight, service, and satisfac-
> tion. God's offer of satisfaction is unique.
> God's offer of satisfaction is unique in its *price.* "Come ye
> to the waters, and he that hath no money; come ye, buy,
> and eat . . . without money and without price" (55:1).
> They are invited to buy wine (gladness) and milk (nour-
> ishment).
> God's offer of satisfaction is unique in its *proposition.* The

invitation is made without restriction. Man's part is summarized by six action verbs of simplicity.

God's offer of satisfaction is unique in its *provision*. The provision is made for their going forth with joy and peace (55:12).

This whole offer of guaranteed satisfaction is centered in the person of the Lord. "Seek ye the LORD while he may be found, call ye upon him while he is near" (55:6). When the wicked turns from his way and the unrighteous man forsakes his thoughts, and they return to the Lord, then the Lord will have mercy and will pardon the sin (55:7). The Saviour holds the key to satisfaction. If you want guaranteed satisfaction, accept Christ as Saviour and let Him be the Lord of your life.

### THE DISCOVERY OF PROBLEMS

There are several means whereby the preacher may discover problems on which he may preach.

One of the best is through *pastoral calling*. Pastoral calling should never be viewed as an appendix to the ministry, but rather as a very vital corollary to it. It is through calling that we learn the specific needs of our people. If a man is going to preach to personal needs, it is necessary that he know what those needs are. This means pastoral work. However, if a man merely reads books, he may become a scholar; but if he separates himself from people, he will never become a preacher. We can bring about uplifting and stablizing influence and encourage our people to share such an encouragement with others within the church.

*Hospital visitation* will also enlighten the pastor regarding problems on which his people need special guidance and help. He will encourage the patient to speak about the things which matter most. He will try to assure the person of God's healing power, love, care, and presence.

As he carries on *conversations with his parishioners after services*, problems will present themselves. He will seek guidance from the Holy Spirit for dealing with these at a later time either through counseling outside the pulpit or counseling through preaching.

He will want to pay attenion to *questions raised by the young people* within the church. These questions will often indicate areas of special need and concern. One national evangelist holding meetings at the Paladium in Hollywood, California, restricted the audience to those between fifteen and twenty-five years of age. Slips of paper and pencils were distributed and the young people were asked to write a question which they would like to have answered. These were used as bases for messages on the succeeding evenings of the campaign.

*Times of emergency* provide topics dealing with special needs.

*Newspapers, weekly magazines, and digests* will also give the sermonizer an indication of those concerns which are foremost in the thinking of the people of his day.

As the sermonizer studies his *Bible,* he should keep in mind some of the problems of his people; he will thereby seek to find some biblical help to share with his congregation as he deals with the problems. It would be wise for him to formulate a list of problems. Then, as he reads his Bible, he should put biblical references under these problems so that he will have the information ready at times when needed.

### SOME TYPICAL PROBLEMS

| | | |
|---|---|---|
| adultery | despondency | guilt feelings |
| adversity | disappointment | handicaps |
| affliction | discouragement | hypocrisy |
| anger | dishonesty | immorality |
| anxiety | disobedience | impatience |
| apathy | divided loyalties | inconsistency |
| backsliding | divorce | indifference |
| complacency | doubt | inferiority |
| compromise | envy | ingratitude |
| coveteousness | failure | insecurity |
| cowardice | family troubles | intolerance |
| cynicism | fear | irresponsibility |
| death | frustrations | jealousy |
| depression | futility | loneliness |
| despair | gossip | lying |

| | | |
|---|---|---|
| nervousness | resentment | temptation |
| poverty | ridicule | tension |
| prejudice | self-control, lack of | unhappiness |
| presumption | selfishness | weariness |
| pride | sorrow | worry |
| procrastination | suffering | zeal, misguided |
| profanity | temper | |

### DANGERS CONNECTED WITH SUCH PREACHING

There are several *dangers* which seem to be especially connected with this type of problem preaching.

1. One of the prominent dangers is connected with the violation of confidence. The sermonizer must beware of this temptation.
2. As he deals with the problem from the pulpit, he must beware of handling it inadequately; for to deal with the problem in such a fashion may do far more damage than good.
3. He must remember that to merely talk about a problem does not solve the problem.
4. There is also the danger of substituting psychology for Christianity.
5. He must never come to the point where he feels that this kind of preaching will take the place of pastoral care. The two go hand in hand.
6. This type of preaching has an attraction for the preacher; therefore, the sermonizer should beware lest he fall into the trap of preaching only this kind of sermon. Too much of this kind of preaching may force the people to give too little attention to God and His provisions for them.
7. Because of the abundance of the materials available to the preacher from extrabiblical sources which deal with each type of problem, he should beware of the danger of allowing biblical content to be crowded out of the sermon.
8. An overemphasis on problem or life-situation preaching could make the preacher wholly occupied with the issues of time, rather than with issues of eternity. He would thereby become merely timely, but not timeless.

9.  There is the danger of this kind of sermon resulting in being a mild editorial comment on a problem, with only a religious flavor to the content.
10. The sermonizer must beware of setting himself up as a psychoanalyst, rather than guiding those with needs to professional help.
11. There is the danger of starting a sermon on the discussion of a problem for which the sermonizer has no solution.
12. Too many problem-centered sermons may put problems into people's minds—problems which were not there previously. A listener may begin to imagine the symptoms of the problem under discussion.
13. There is always the danger of dealing with a problem which is not actually faced by the local congregation.
14. There is the danger also of providing instruction and illustration without personal application.
15. There is the danger of having such an emphasis upon problem preaching that he will exclude doctrinal preaching to the detriment of his congregation.
16. There is the danger of preaching an incomplete life-situation sermon by not bringing man to the cross for pardon and to the living Christ for life-giving power.
17. There is the danger of confusing Christian morality with natural virtue.
18. The final danger is that the preacher's message may be distorted by some emotional need of his own, demanding satisfaction. He should ask himself, "Am I preaching on the needs of my people or on my own needs?"

## General Requirements

If one is going to preach to human needs, he must saturate himself with the content of the Scriptures. Someone has said that every need known to man is described in the Bible. There's the jealousy of Saul, the loyalty of Jonathan, the courage of Nathan, the despair of Jeremiah and the struggles of Paul. There was Jacob beset with the malady of a guilty conscience. God had a cure for this in Genesis 32:22-32. There was Elijah and his problem of his discouragement. God had cure for him in 1 Kings

19:1-18. There was Job with his question regarding the meaning of suffering. God had an answer for him as He put him through the "school of suffering," especially in Job 42. Isaiah was troubled by despondency, but God had an answer for him in Isaiah 6. Daniel faced the problem of maintaining godliness in the midst of ungodly surroundings. His secret whereby this problem could be met and overcome is recorded in Daniel 6.

Every emotion experienced by man is described in the Psalms—crippling emotions such as guilt, doubt, futility, and fear. Also, there is found the assurance of forgiveness, the belief in the value of the individual, the challenge to self-forgetting service, the message of the transforming power of love, and an unquestioning, unfaltering faith which makes life strong and gives it meaning.

One of the chief requirements for the sermonizer who is to preach on problems is that he has what R. H. Edwards has called "person-mindedness." When he can sense the supreme significance of persons in our world, when he can get them into central focus, and when they count above everything else—only then can he be possessed with "person-mindedness." Only then can he have one of the first prerequisites for being an effective Christian preacher upon the problems of his people.

The following poem points up this need in an interesting fashion.

> A parish-priest of austerity,
> Climbed up in a high Church-steeple
> To be nearer God, that he might hand
> His Word down to the people.
> And in sermon-script he daily wrote
> What he *thought* was sent from heaven,
> And dropped it down on the people's heads
> Two times one day in seven!
> In his age, God said, "Come down and die,"
> And he cried out from his steeple,
> "Where art Thou, Lord?" and the Lord replied,
> "Down here among My people!"[14]

### SUGGESTED METHODS FOR CONSTRUCTING SERMONS

The sermonizer now faces the task of constructing a sermon

which will discuss the problem in terms of daily living and scriptural revelation in order that he, the preacher, may share with his people a possible cure or solution. One homiletics writer has suggested that we use a four-point message in dealing with a problem through preaching. The four points would be

1. Where are we?          3. Where do we want to go?
2. How did we get here?   4. How do we get there?

Another writer has suggested three points; namely,

1. The problem—this is the situation.
2. The principle—this is the basis on which it may be solved.
3. The program—this is the way to solve it.

I would suggest a type of sermon which combines the process of reflective thinking, as evidenced in the writings of John Dewey, and the discussion method, together with a strong emphasis upon a solution to the problem as set forth in the Word of God.

Dewey, in his *Process of Reflective Thinking*, suggested that there are five steps:

Step one:    A felt difficulty
Step two:    Its location and definition
Step three:  The suggestion of a possible solution
Step four:   The development by reasoning of the bearings of the suggestion
Step five:   The further observation and experiment leading to its acceptance of belief or disbelief

A *discussion method* has been developed for directing thought in the discussion of a problem. This discussion method involves an adaptation of Dewey's analysis. An outline of this discussion method by McBurney and Hance includes five steps.[15]

Step one: "The Definition and Delimitation of the Problem." Reflective thinking has its inception in some kind of felt difficulty, perplexing situation or problem. Our task is first to locate the problem as definitely as possible.

Step two: "The Analyzing of the Problem." This is an attempt to find out what is wrong and what is causing the trouble. It is an attempt to discover the nature of the problem in terms of its causal relationships.

Step three: "The Suggestions of Hypotheses or Solutions." By a solution we merely mean an hypothesis or a proposal which is offered tentatively as a possible cure or suggestion.

Step four: "The Reasoned Development of the Hypotheses or Solutions in the Preceeding Step." This includes a weighing and comparing of the relative merits in terms of the causes of the problem.

Step five: "Further Verification." It is profitable for a group to review carefully the steps that they will need to take in putting the proposed solutions into operation.

### The Sermonic Process of Investigation

Having noted Dewey's steps in reflective thinking, and that which discussion theory has developed based upon these steps of reflective thinking, we have tried to establish a sermon outline pattern. The aim of this outline is to discuss the problem together with our listeners in such a way that they will see the problem, realize some of the suggested solutions which have been advanced, and then come to realize what the Bible has to offer toward a cure or solution. The sermon process combines some of the features of reflective thinking and the discussion method within a biblically oriented sermon structure. This sermonic process we call *the process of investigation.*

Biblical preaching has several unique purposes which distinguish it from the general discussion of a problem in secular terms. The discussion process has therefore been adjusted to meet the needs of the biblical sermon. The outstanding feature of change is the special emphasis placed upon the biblical solution to the problem.

Just as there were eight steps in the basic sermon plan in the process of modification, so there are eight steps to follow in this process of investigation. These eight steps are the following:

> Step one:     Determine the subject
> Step two:     Select a theme
> Step three:   Formulate a proposition

Step four:      Establish a transitional sentence
Step five:      Develop main divisions
Step six:       Amplify main divisions into subdivisions
Step seven:  Formulate an introduction
Step eight:    Formulate a conclusion

We now proceed to identify and exemplify each of these eight points as they pertain to the investigation sermonic process. The *subject* is the broad or general problem area. In terms of the sample outline based upon 1 Kings 19, the subject would be "Discouragement." The *theme* combines with this subject a limitation which indicates the particular emphasis of this sermon. The theme will always be a phrase. In our present illustration, the theme would be "Overcoming Discouragement." The *proposition* is interrogative in form since it states the problem for which a solution, cure, or answer is sought. This interrogative sentence should be concise and clear. It is the core of the entire sermon. The proposition for the example which we are developing might be "How can a Christian overcome discouragement?" This proposition appears on the investigation outline as the fourth main point. The fourth step in the process of construction is the establishment of a *transitional sentence*. This transitional sentence will transform the interrogative proposition into a declarative statement. The sentence will also include an interrogative or interrogative substitute and a keyword. This means that this transitional sentence for an investigation sermon will include the same elements as any transitional sentence used in a modification sermon. This emphasizes the fact that the fourth segment of the investigation outline is a modification sermon in miniature. An example of a transitional sentence which might be used in a sermon based upon 1 Kings 19 might be "A Christian can overcome discouragement by following the steps outlined in 1 Kings 19:1-18." This transitional sentence appears in the sermon outline immediately after the explanation in the final outline.

Before going beyond this point, let us view the first four steps of sermon construction in respect to their relationship to one another.

*Subject:* Discouragement
*Theme:* Overcoming Discouragement
*Proposition:* How can a Christian overcome discouragement?
*Transitional Sentence:* A Christian can overcome discouragement by following the steps outlined in 1 Kings 19:1-18.

We turn now to the second group of steps. *Step five* involves the formulation of the main points. Since this investigation procedure has been patterned after the discussion method employed in secular speech work, we have designated the number and nature of the points to be included in this outline. There will be four main points and each of these will be given in the form of a question.

  I. *What is the problem?*
 II. *How prevalent is the problem?*
III. *What have been some of the proposed solutions to the problem?*
 IV. (The interrogative proposition)

The *sixth step* in sermon construction involves the amplification of the main points and thereby getting subpoints or arabics. The *first main point,* "What is the problem?" can be developed by defining, limiting, and diagnosing the problem. The definition of the problem might be by negation, classification, etymology, context, illustration, or by giving synonyms. The limitation of the problem might come because of the character of the audience, the occasion, and the possible area of its application. The problem might be diagnosed by giving symptoms, causes, and effects. The sermonizer must be certain that there is a concise statement of the problem given as part of this point. The *second main point* reads, "How prevalent is the problem?" As the sermonizer expands and develops this point, he will note first of all the prevalence of the problem in reading, listening, and the working experiences of the preacher and his people. The development will then show the occurrence of the problem in Scripture as a whole and in specific sections of Scripture. The listener should realize after hearing the development of this section of the sermon that since it is so prevalent, we should be concerned with it.

By giving specifics, the sermonizer is attempting to establish an evident need for dealing with the problem. The *third main point* reads, "What have been some of the proposed solutions to the problem?" This can be developed by giving at least two solutions which have been advanced by extrabiblical sources. The source, nature, and sponsor of each proposal should be noted. This will enable the listener to check for himself at a later date if he so desires. It will also show the listener that the preacher has done some research on the problem before attempting to preach upon it. A fair evaluation of each extrabiblical solution and proposal will be given by the sermonizer. The sermonizer should seek to formulate an identifying label for each proposal. The *fourth main point* is the proposition. This gives the problem in interrogative form thus setting the stage for seeking a solution within the scriptures. The sermonic explanation should appear in the outline between the proposition and the transitional sentence. This serves to orient the listener to the relationship of the passage to the problem. The transitional sentence as described previously appears after the explanation. Each of the subdivisions should be characterized by the keyword which appears in the transitional sentence. The amount of development listed under each subdivision will depend upon the amount of time at the disposal of the preacher.

The *seventh step* to be developed in the process of preparation is the *introduction*. There will be a strong emphasis upon the presence of the problem in the daily experience of the listeners and the preacher. What prompted the preacher to give consideration to this problem as the basis for the sermon? Is this problem receiving national attention? Have magazines and newspapers been dealing with this problem recently? The introduction should be concise and specific. A visual aid may be used at this point by bringing an actual news item into the pulpit for reading.

The *eighth step* is the formulation of the *conclusion*. This will emphasize the applications and general development of the fourth section of the message which includes the biblical approach and proposals for a solution, cure, or answer to the problem. This message should conclude with a motion. The listener should face a decision at this point. He should be challenged to put the biblical solution, cure, or answer into practice. Teikmanis has suggested that authentic preaching is a celebration of God-given victory over the crises of life.[16] The victory is always from God. The preacher should make certain that God gets the glory for providing the cure.

Preachers have a unique professional privilege in that they appear before the people several times each week to speak to them of the real issues of life. What other professional person has such a privilege? Whether the preacher begins with the needs of the people and moves with them into the Scriptures or begins with the scriptures and moves out to their needs is not a matter of great concern. In either case, he must know their needs and he must know the Scriptures.

### THE SERMONIC PROCESS OF INVESTIGATION IN CONTRAST TO THE MODIFICATION PROCESS

Two sample sermon outlines have been included. The first of these deals with 1 Kings 19 making use of the *modification* sermonic process. This type of sermon would be especially suited to the traditional, biblically oriented congregation. The second sample sermon is based upon the *investigation* process. It will be especially useful when facing a university audience or professionally oriented audience or congregation. They have been conditioned to consider a discussion approach to problems. This is the process which has been outlined in this segment of material. Please note the fact that the body of the *modification* sermon in condensed form is the substance of the fourth section of the *investigation* sermon.

May it be, as we present scriptural answers to man's perplexities that many who listen may be stirred to say as God speaks to them through His message,

> I will say of the LORD, He is
> my refuge and my fortress: my
> God; in him will I trust.
>
> PSALM 91:2

## SAMPLE SERMON OUTLINE—MODIFICATION

PREACHING PORTION: 1 Kings 19:1-18
SERMONIC PROCESS: Modification
SUBJECT: Discouragement
THEME: Overcoming discouragement

### A Cure for Discouragement

INTRODUCTION

*Approach Sentence:* "All discouragement is from the devil" (Quote from Catherine Marshall).

*Outlined Portion*

　1. Discouragement and our daily living
　2.

*Explanation*

　1. (Show relationship between 1 Kings and discouragement).
　2. (Show the prevalence of discouragement within the Scriptures).

PROPOSITION: A Christian can overcome discouragement.

TRANSITIONAL SENTENCE: A Christian can overcome discouragement by following the steps outlined in 1 Kings 19:1-18.

　I. *Make certain that you are prepared physically.* 1 Kings 19:4-8— "And he arose, and did eat and drink, and went in the strength of that meat forty days and forty nights" (v. 8).
　　1.
　　(Illustration)
　　2. (Show how the truth of the main point may be applied to the immediate congregation).

　II. *Make certain that you are prepared spiritually.* 1 Kings 19:9-14— "And after the fire a still small voice" (v. 12*b*): "What doest thou here, Elijah?" (v. 13*b*).
　　1.
　　2.
　　(Illustration)
　　3. (Show how the truth of the main point may be applied to the immediate congregation).

　III. *Make certain that you are involved in service.* 1 Kings 19:15-18— "And the LORD said unto him, Go, return on thy way to the wilderness of Damascus" (v. 15).

    1.

    2.

    (Illustration)

    3.  (Show how the truth of the main point may be applied to the immediate congregation).

  IV. *Make certain that you are ready to work with others.* 1 Kings 19:19-21—"So he departed thence, and found Elisha . . . and cast his mantle upon him" (v. 19).

    (Illustration)

    1.

    2.  (Show how the truth of the main point may be applied to the immediate congregation).

CONCLUSION: Therefore, we as Christians should take the necessary steps to overcome discouragement:

| | |
|---|---|
| 1.  Get ready physically. | 3.  Get involved in service. |
| 2.  Get ready spiritually. | 4.  Be ready to work with others. |

## SAMPLE SERMON OUTLINE—INVESTIGATION

PREACHING PORTION: 1 Kings 19:1-18

SERMONIC PROCESS: Investigation

SUBJECT: Discouragement

THEME: Overcoming discouragement

### A Cure for Discouragement

INTRODUCTION: Discouragement seems to vary in direct ratio and proportion to the frequency with which we follow local and national news.

    1.

    2.

  I. *What is the problem?*

    1. How would you define it? "Discouragement is the stage of being depressed, dejected and hopeless" *(American College Dictionary).*

    2. What are its limits, effects and possible cause?

  II. *How prevalent is the problem?*

    1. In Scripture.

    2. In present day living.

 III. *What have been some of the proposed solutions to the problem?* (Each subpoint will be a proposed solution.)

1. Where did you read or hear about the proposed solution?
2. Who advocates it?
3. What do you think of its merits or weaknesses?

IV. *How can a Christian overcome discouragement?*
Explanation: (Show the relationship between the problem and the passage—in this case 1 Kings 19:1-18.)

TRANSITIONAL SENTENCE: A Christian can overcome discouragement by following the steps outlined in 1 Kings 19:1-18.

1. *Make certain that you are physically prepared.* 1 Kings 19:4-8. "And he arose, and did eat and drink, and went in the strength of that meat forty days and forty nights" (v. 8).
(Insert subpoints.)

2. *Make certain that you are prepared spiritually.* 1 Kings 19:9-14. "And after the fire a still small voice" (v. 12b). "What doest thou here, Elijah?" (v. 13b).
(Insert subpoints.)

3. *Make certain that you are involved in service.* 1 Kings 19:15-18. "And the LORD said unto him, Go, return thy way to the wilderness of Damascus" (v. 15).
(Insert subpoints.)

4. *Make certain that you are ready to work with others.* 1 Kings 19:19-21. "So he departed thence, and found Elisha . . . and cast his mantle upon him" (v. 19).
(Insert subpoints.)

CONCLUSION: Therefore, we as Christians should take these steps as outlined in 1 Kings 19 in order that we might overcome discouragement.

1. Get ready physically.          3. Get involved in service.
2. Get ready spiritually.         4. Be ready to work with others.

## Reading List

Blackwood, A. W. *The Preparation of Sermons.* Nashville: Abingdon-Cokesbury, 1946.

Bowie, Walter R. *Preaching.* New York: Abingdon, 1954.

Brastow, Lewis O. *The Work of the Preacher.* Boston: Pilgrim, 1914.

Caldwell, Frank. *Preaching Angles.* Nashville: Abingdon, 1954.

Cleland, James T. *Preaching to be Understood.* Nashville: Abingdon, 1965.

Coffin, Henry Sloane. *What to Preach.* New York: Doran, 1926.

Dargan, Edwin Charles. *A History of Preaching*. 3 vol. New York: Doran, 1905.

Gibson, George Miles. *Planned Preaching*. Philadelphia: Westminster, 1954.

Jefferson, Charles. *The Minister as a Prophet*. New York: Crowell, 1905.

————. *The Minister as a Shepherd*. New York: Crowell, 1912.

Jordan, Gerald Ray. *You Can Preach*. New York: Revell, 1951.

Kemp, Charles F. *Life Situation Preaching*. St. Louis: Bethany, 1958.

Linn, Edmund H. *Preaching as Counseling*. Valley Forge: Judson, 1960.

Luccock, Halford E. *In the Minister's Workshop*. New York: Abingdon-Cokesbury, 1944.

MacGregor, W. M. *The Making of a Preacher*. Philadelphia: Westminster, 1946.

MacLennan, David. *Pastoral Preaching*. Philadelphia: Westminster, 1955.

McBurney, J. H., and Hance, K. G. *Discussion in Human Affairs*. New York: Harper, 1950.

McCracken, Robert. *The Making of the Sermon*. New York: Harper, 1956.

McNeil, Jesse Jai. *The Preacher-Prophet in Mass Society*. Grand Rapids: Eerdmans, 1961.

Meyer, F. B. *Expository Preaching: Plans and Methods*. New York: Doran, 1912.

Oates, Wayne. *The Christian Pastor*. Philadelphia: Westminster, 1951.

Sleeth, Ronald E. *Proclaiming the Word*. Nashville: Abingdon, 1964.

Smith, Charles. *Biblical Authority for Modern Preaching*. Philadelphia: Westminster, 1960.

Teikmanis, Arthur L. *Preaching and Pastoral Care*. Englewood Cliffs: Prentice-Hall, 1964.

Tizard, J. L. *Preaching, the Art of Communication*. London: Oxford, 1958.

Webber, F. R. *A History of Preaching in Britain and America*. 3 vol. Milwaukee: Northwestern, 1953.

# 6

## Biblical Preaching
## and Doctrinal Communication

IT WAS CHARLES G. FINNEY who made the statement many years ago that there has never been a revival that was not brought about by doctrine, set forth with power and clearness. This same truth can be enforced by a quotation given by Phillips Brooks.

> No preaching ever had any strong power that was not the preaching of doctrine. The preachers that have moved and held men have always preached doctrine. No exhortation to a good life that does not put behind it some truth as deep as eternity can seize and hold the conscience. Preach doctrine, preach all the doctrine that you know, and learn forever more and more; but preach it always, not that men may believe it, but that men may be saved by believing it. So it shall be live, not dead. So men shall rejoice in it and not decry it. So they shall feed on it at your hands as on the bread of life, solid and sweet, and claiming for itself the appetite which God made for it.[1]

Andrew Blackwood stated that "in the past every evangelistic movement blessed of God has come largely through preaching doctrine."[2] The preaching which omits doctrine is preaching which is deficient in one of the most important constituents. Where the pulpit is weak in its doctrinal presentation, the congregation lacks spiritual strength.

### THE NATURE OF DOCTRINAL PREACHING

The question may well be raised at this point as to what we mean by doctrinal preaching. *Doctrinal preaching* is preaching which aims at instructing the people methodically in the truths of the gospel. The business of theological preaching is to answer the most basic questions men are capable of asking. The doctrine of God answers whether or not the universe is friendly, and whether life has purpose and meaning. The doctrine of man tells us whether or not man is able to apprehend the meaning of life and to ally himself with God in fellowship and service. The doctrine of salvation answers man's question as to how life can be redeemed from frustration and futility and lifted to its highest levels. The emphasis within the doctrinal sermon will be more upon truths than upon duties. This does not mean however that a doctrinal sermon is merely a theological treatise. It is not the exposition of one or more doctrines irrespective of how important the doctrine may be. The doctrinal sermon is first of all a sermon, after that it is a doctrinal sermon. As a sermon it combines exposition with application.

The decline in doctrinal preaching is not wholly due to a decline of interest in doctrine. It is partly due to the difficulty which we who preach have in handling doctrine within the context of a sermon.

### The Advantages of Doctrinal Preaching

There are many advantages to be gained through doctrinal preaching. Such preaching certainly gives honor to the gospel. It instructs and edifies the listener. It adds to the intellectual character of the ministry. It clears up difficulties which have gathered in the minds of the listeners in respect to important truths and facts of Christianity. Such preaching helps the listener discriminate between that which is primary and that which is secondary in Christian truth. It provides a firm foundation for effective ethical preaching.

### The Objections to Doctrinal Preaching

Several objections have been raised to doctrinal preaching. It is objected that the essential articles of Christian doctrine are plain and few, and that since these are sufficient for salvation we should not labor so hard at trying to preach a great number of doctrinal truths. Some labor the point that doctrinal preaching lacks the warmth and animation which should characterize sermons. Others have stated that in their opinion doctrinal preaching disturbs and perplexes the hearers, thereby hampering their edification rather than helping it. Another objection states that doctrinal preaching occasions doubtful disputations and strife over words. It has been objected that doctrinal sermons are dry. We must admit that doctrinal sermons are often dry, but this is not the fault of doctrine but of the preacher.

M. Reu, lists three ways of making doctrinal sermons dry. (I should mention at this point that some preachers do not have to work at this, it seems to come naturally.) He states that doctrinal sermons become dry whenever they enter into subtle distinctions of dogmatics and forget the difference between the technical knowledge of the specialist in theology and the saving knowledge of the Christian congregation. The second cause of dryness in the doctrinal sermon is its failure to bring the truth it treats to bear on practical life. The final way noted by Reu is to forget that one is to preach and therefore merely be presenting a dissertation rather than trying to convey truth to living hearers before him with whom he is to enter into personal and living contact.[3] There is no sure way to prevent the minds of the listeners from wandering, but if we translate the gospel into understandable language our cause will be helped. We must strive to reveal the relationship of the doctrine to Christian life and experience. The preacher must therefore always be on the alert for ways of presenting old truths in new ways.

## An Historical Survey of Doctrinal Preaching

A survey of the history of doctrinal preaching both chronologically and biographically will serve to highlight the pinnacles of doctrinal preaching and some of the preachers who have scaled the heights. It will also point out some of the low points. An interesting study could be pursued in an attempt to show the possible correlation between the strength and weakness of the church and the corresponding emphasis upon doctrinal preaching within particular periods.

The preaching in the Apostolic Period (4 B.C.–A.D. 69) included the preaching by Jesus and the apostles. This preaching was noted for simplicity, picturesqueness, versatility, practicality, optimism, the use of Scripture, and the tone of authority. There was an intermingling of doctrine and ethics.

The preaching in the Patristic Period (70-430) became more systematic in form. There was a growing appeal to human opinion rather than to the Word of God. The fourth century is remembered as a period of great preaching.

The preaching of the Early Medieval Period (430-1095) is remembered for its emphasis upon the sacraments and missionary outreach. During the seventh and eighth centuries allegorizing was rampant and the faithful exposition of the scripture was almost nonexistent. During this period there was very little emphasis upon the doctrine of the atonement.

The preaching of the Central Medieval Period (1095-1300) was popular in tone but dealt more with legends than with the scriptures. Scholasticism and mysticism were emphasized during this period.

The preaching of the Renaissance and Late Medieval Period (1300-1500) could be characterized as being in a state of decay. This was in contrast to the thirteenth century, which had been one of the high points in preaching. A reformatory note did begin to make itself felt in this period, as seen in the preaching of John Wycliff.

The preaching in the Reformation Period (1500-1572) was from the heart and had as its primary purpose the stirring of the people to faith. The sixteenth century was one of the three high points of preaching. The other two were the fourth and the thirteenth centuries.

The preaching in the Early Modern Period (1572-1789) has been remembered for the force it exerted upon national life. The period has been remembered as the "Golden Age of English Preaching."

The preaching of the Late Modern Period (1789-1900) was basically Calvinistic and scholarly. The Puritan sermons were treatises on theology.

The preaching of the twentieth century emphasized social

reform, life-situation preaching, and a decline in doctrinal content.

## A BIOGRAPHICAL SURVEY OF DOCTRINAL PREACHING

These men have been regarded as noteworthy preachers of doctrine. By studying their lives, we gain information regarding the factors which God uses in developing a doctrinal preacher. By reading their sermons, we see examples of sermons arranged for presentation which God has blessed in past days. The study of their lives and the reading of their sermons should provide inspiration and information for the improvement of doctrinal preaching.

JOHN WYCLIFF (1328-84) has been referred to as the "Morning Star" of the Reformation. His preaching became an instrument of spiritual warfare. Through his preaching, doctrine became the possession of people. His approach was intellectual but practical.

MARTIN LUTHER (1483-1546) constantly emphasized in his preaching the fact that duty was founded upon doctrine. His first appeal was to scripture and then to reason. He was a man of the Bible and is remembered for having translated it into German. His preaching included a strong emphasis upon the doctrines of repentence and faith.

JOHN CALVIN (1509-54) was one of the outstanding preachers of all time. He made careful preparation for his preaching and in a fifteen-year period preached 3,000 sermons without notes or manuscript. He was a biblical preacher and noted for sound doctrine. He used his theological learning to clarify the meaning of the words of Scripture.

LANCELOT ANDREWS (1555-1626) was the Bishop of Chichester. In his preaching he kept close to the text and used the main divisions of the text as the main divisions of his messages. We remember him as being one of the translators of the King James version.

JOHN DONNE (1573-1631) incorporated a clear exposition of the doctrine of redemption.

THOMAS GOODWIN (1600-1680) became a Christian after he had pastored a church for some years. He resolved to preach sound words without affectation of wit and vanity of eloquence. His sermons give evidence of unction. His expositions are minute and diffuse.

JEREMY TAYLOR (1613-67) has been referred to both as a "poet" of the pulpit and also as the "Shakespeare" of the divines. His greatest strength lay in his devotional works. Some have said that he was one of the most gifted churchmen and theologians of England. Doctrine entered his preaching but probably he should not be referred to as a strong doctrinal preacher. It has been said that he would be a dangerous model but a delightful companion.

RICHARD BAXTER (1615-91) used themes in his preaching which were largely theological. He persuaded men to study and to live according to the essential doctrines of Christianity. He made a powerful impression upon his times and remains today as the best known of the Puritan preachers.

JOHN OWEN (1616-83) and THEODORE CUYLER (1822-90) might be added to this list.

JOHN BUNYAN (1628-88) became one of the most eminent preachers of his generation. Thousands flocked to hear his popular presentations. He was a man of intense faith and is especially remembered as the author of *Pilgrim's Progress*.

JOHN HOWE (1630-1705) emphasized practical pastoral experiences and the regular study of the Scriptures. He wrote many doctrinal treatises, and called upon his people to recall the cardinal doctrines of the gospel.

JOHN KNOX (1505-72) came under Calvin's influence when exiled to Geneva. He then took Calvinism to Scotland. Historians have said that he made a more lasting impact upon his nation's destiny than all others whose lives played a part in its formative years. He was a man of emphatic convictions. He was a courageous reformer with a powerful delivery. The records show that he preached on an average of five times a week to overflow congregations.

An evangelical awakening broke out in several countries including America, Wales, England, and Scotland. The preachers of this era preached two or three times a day seven days a week in an itinerant ministry. They preached the law with severity. Their basic message was Jesus Christ crucified, the only hope of man's salvation. Their sermons, however, lacked much in terms of theology and were generally topical. Their printed sermons are serious, carefully written, and generally impressive. The preachers of the Awakening came to close grips with their hearers, which caused many to lift their voices in confession of sin and to cry out for salvation. Preaching gradually changed and the Bible became central in preaching. The new form of sermon with its emphasis on man's sin and his redemption through the Lord Jesus became the rule rather than the rare exception. Two of the outstanding preachers of this period were:

JOHN WESLEY (1703-91) who was a theologian and doctrinal preacher. The theology which he preached was the standard theology of Methodism for more than 150 years. He expounded the doctrines because of their practical value to the hearers. It has been said that he preached 18,000 sermons in 34 years. Wesley emphasized the work of the Holy Spirit.

GEORGE WHITEFIELD (1714-70) in his preaching emphasized the doctrines of sanctification and election. His sermons led to strong calls to repentance. His doctrinal emphasis was strongly Calvinistic.

As the clergymen in England and Scotland arrived at certain truths through their study of the Word of God, they preached sin and grace with power. Doctrinal preaching increased. Not only was there an emphasis on sin and grace but also on repentance and faith. The need for individual salvation was seen. The law and the gospel were preached, but the distinction between the two was not always clear. This evangelical group exerted a great influence in England even though they were in a minority. The following seven preachers might be studied in connection with this group:

ANDREW FULLER (1754-1815) was one of the supporters of William Carey.

CHARLES SIMEON (1759-1836) emphasized the preaching of the doctrine of redemption. He presented stirring Christ-centered sermons. It was his feeling that the Bible was the ultimate source of appeal in the exposition of doctrine. He was Calvinistic in his approach.

ROBERT HALL (1764-1831) possessed the ability to present the evangelical doctrines in an attractive way. His sermons included the ability to present an intense and ardent application of the doctrines. His sermons are mostly topical though while he was at Cambridge he often delivered expository sermons.

WILLIAM JAY (1769-1831) preached sermons which were a combination of doctrinal, experiential, and practical. He said that the best preaching was doctrinal, combined with the practice of the gospel. It was his feeling that in preaching doctrine it was better that many things be assumed rather than be technically discussed within the sermon.

RICHARD WATSON (1737-1816) was one of the formulators of the Methodist Theological System as set forth in his work *Theological Institutes*. The special emphasis in his preaching was centered upon the crucifixion of Christ.

THOMAS CHALMERS (1780-1847) was possibly the greatest preacher of the 19th century and also one of the greatest soul-winners of that century. He was minister at Glasgow and professor at St. Andrews and Edinburgh.

THOMAS BINNEY (1798-1874) was especially noted for what we now term life-situation preaching. He was also at home with theological questions and sought to make the Scriptures vital to the people.

During the period of the nineteenth century many of the old evils began to reappear in the churches. Preaching began to lose its evangelical fervor, especially in the Anglican church. There was the substitution of an "infallible" intellect for an infallible book. Many controversies arose, one of which established the right of the clergymen to believe and preach doctrines not in harmony with those of the established church and without fear of doctrinal discipline. Another declared that a clergyman is not obliged to accept every part of the Bible as inspired nor to believe that Christ's merit can be imputed to the believer, nor to doubt that the wicked are eternally punished. Preaching began to lack clarity because of the inroads of destructive biblical criticism.

In the Anglican church there was a gradual departure from the doctrinal preaching of Puritan days and from the exposition of the great principles of the plan of salvation such as was found in the days of the Great Awakening. Sermons tended to become essays. They were topical rather than textual or expository. The church was looked at as the court of last resort rather than the Bible. Some of the preachers of this period whose contributions might be studied include:

F. W. ROBERTSON (1816-53) was an expository preacher whose sermons were both scriptural and practical. His method was to begin to construct each sermon by first using a text, probe for its meaning, draw its meaning out into expository form, then draw doctrine from it. His sermons were normally about 45 minutes in length. He knew the New Testament by heart both in English and in Greek. His life's motto was "None but Christ."

H. P. LIDDON (1829-90) preached doctrinal messages with a sacramental emphasis. He is especially remembered for his series preaching on the divinity of Christ.

R. W. DALE (1829-95) was recognized as the great doctrinal preacher of the nineteenth century. His sermons were doctrinal in emphasis and expository in method. He was a nonconformist and worked in Carr's Lane Congregational Church for 42 years.

JOSEPH PARKER (1830-1902) as a preacher was gifted with many qualities such as depth of conviction, intensity of feeling, and energy of utterance. He enjoyed setting forth the truth in continuous exposition. He employed both expository and topical sermons. There was a special emphasis within his preaching on the love of Jesus Christ. He believed in and preached justification by faith.

CHARLES H. SPURGEON (1834-92) has been referred to as the "Preacher's Preacher." He was a Puritan Calvinist, holding to the doctrine of covenants. His stand was conditioned by commitment to believer's baptism.

PETER T. FORSYTH (1849-1921) preached doctrinal messages especially centered upon the cross and the love of God.

CHARLES BROWN'S (1862-1930) messages were Christ-centered and employed an expository method. He treated all doctrine in terms of its scriptural foundations. He is especially remembered for his preaching in the college chapel.

JOHN D. JONES (1797-1840) used the expository method and stressed redemption in Christ, forgiveness of sin and the immortality of the soul.

## A SURVEY OF DOCTRINAL PREACHERS IN AMERICA

A study of several preachers will provide an unfolding panorama of information covering doctrinal preaching on the American continent. Some of these men might be:

COTTON MATHER (1663-1728) who preached on the mediatorial work of the Saviour and the influence of the Holy Spirit. He thought preachers should study theology because they basically present the doctrine of grace in their sermons. His sermons were based on doctrine, but he was not free from doctrinal error.

JONATHAN EDWARDS (1703-58) is famous for his sermon "Sinners in the Hands of an Angry God." He gave special attention to objective doctrines in his sermons.

TIMOTHY DWIGHT (1752-1817) had a firm faith in the evangelical doctrines. He employed this sound doctrine in his preaching and produced good models of doctrinal discourse.

LYMAN BEECHER (1775-1863) preached doctrinal sermons and applied them in a practical manner. He presented the ethical aspects of Christianity without sacrificing doctrine. His logic was that of an intellectual giant. His homiletical style was so smooth that one hardly realized the presence of main divisions.

W. E. CHANNING (1780-1842) was a doctrinal preacher though he was not an evangelical. His doctrinal preaching was applied to life situations being strong on ethical considerations.

HORACE BUSHNELL (1802-76) sought to restore reality to accepted theology. He believed strongly that doctrine should be formulated in Christian experience.

CHARLES G. FINNEY (1792-1875) placed a special emphasis upon the deity of Christ. He deserves special and prominent place in the annals of preaching because of his evangelistic emphasis as well as his doctrinal emphasis. There was strong emphasis within his preaching on the vicarious atonement, justification by grace through faith, and the power of the Holy Spirit to transform men.

PHILLIPS BROOKS (1835-93) presented theology in simple, practical ways. He taught doctrine on Wednesday and then preached on Sunday with the basic doctrinal teaching understood.

WASHINGTON GLADDEN (1836-1918) socialized American theology and pushed it toward a liberal stance.

GEORGE GORDON (1853-1929) was an earnest trinitarian theologian who was, however, inclined toward liberal theology.

G. GORE (1853-1932) wrote two books, *The Creed of the Christian* and *Prayer and the Lord's Prayer,* which reveal his power of presenting the doctrinal and existential obligations of Christianity.

CHARLES JEFFERSON (1860-1937) was a doctrinal preacher, but he sought to avoid technical terms. He said that the experience of 1900 years proves that only doctrinal preaching reconciles the heart of a person to God. He felt that practical preaching was doctrinal preaching.

J. G. MACHEN (1887-1937) wrote many books dealing with doctrine. He is remembered as a theologian and New Testament scholar.

DONALD G. BARNHOUSE (1895-1962) was the pastor of the Tenth Presbyterian Church of Philadelphia. He is especially remembered for preaching through the books of the Bible. The systematic theology course constructed around the book of Romans was one of his outstanding contributions.

HAROLD J. OCKENGA (1905-  ) is now the president of Gordon-Conwell schools. He employs expository biblical sermons with an emphasis upon doctrinal themes. The sermons are oriented toward the intellect, rather than toward the emotions.

### SUGGESTIONS FOR DOCTRINAL PREACHING

A survey of sixty-eight homiletics text and trade books written by American-born homiletics teachers in America between 1834 and 1954 shows that twenty-seven of the sixty-eight made reference to doctrinal preaching. Of these twenty-seven about seventeen could be regarded as making major contributions in this area. The two authors devoting the greatest number of pages to this type of preaching were Skinner in his book, *Aids to Revealing and Hearing,* and Brastow in his book, *The Work of the Preacher: A Study of Homiletic Principles and Methods.*[4]

Several helpful suggestions can be gleaned from a reading of these textbooks. Alexander, Johnson, and Brastow all emphasize the fact that the doctrinal material should be presented in light of its surroundings and it should be made practical. Burrell and Fritz emphasize that the preacher should avoid technicalities. Alexander goes on to say that the preacher should not heap up a pile of texts. It was also suggested that the preacher should avoid controversial preaching.

Dabney in his book, *Sacred Rhetoric,* adds three suggestions to the effect that doctrinal preaching should be science-made-popular, it should be understandable and the preacher should attempt to preach all the truth.

Schneck in his book, *Modern Practical Theology,* stresses the need for the preacher to be personally convinced of a doctrine: "He must see it and love it, and his own conscience must be alive to it."

Johnson in his book, *The Ideal Ministry,* encourages the preacher to preach doctrine frequently. The doctrines should be preached in their entirety. The presentations should be adapted to the times of the preacher.

### Types of Doctrinal Sermons

There are several types of doctrinal sermons. Brastow mentions three—the declarative, the apologetic, and the polemical.[5] Apologetics deals with the relationship of the Christian faith to the wider sphere of man's secular knowledge such as philosophy, science, and history, with a view toward showing that faith is not at variance with the truth that these enquiries have uncovered.[6] Polemics deals with the many varieties of opinion, differences, and theories within the Christian church. Broadus felt that the preaching of specific sermons on or about apologetics should be avoided. He was of the opinion that helpful references and statements defending the faith within a general sermon would be helpful. Broadus also felt much the same way about preaching in the area of polemics. This appeared to him to grow out of a love for conflict on the part of the preacher, and he felt that such preaching would often lead to divisions within the group. He felt that the preacher should be mainly occupied with the advocacy of positive truth.

The declarative type of doctrinal sermon mentioned by Brastow would be similar to the sermon of affirmation referred to by Jordan.[7] The main characteristic of this type of sermon is the bringing up to date of the truth which was once presented by our forefathers in dogmatic fashion. Sermons on the creeds are readily adapted to this pattern.

Blackwood made reference to two additional types of doctrinal sermons. They were the direct and the indirect. He selects four sermons by different preachers to illustrate what he means by preaching doctrine indirectly:

> "Every Man's Life a Plan of God"
> (Is 45:5) by Horace Bushnell
> "The Fire and the Calf"
> (Ex 32:24) by Phillips Brooks
> "The Reversal of Human Judgments"
> (Mt 19:30) by James B. Mozley
> "But When Life Tumbles In, What Then?"
> (Jer 12:5) by Arthur J. Gossip[8]

### COLLECTING MATERIAL FOR DOCTRINAL SERMONS

How should we study doctrine as preparation for preaching? We should begin by surveying the scriptures for doctrinal emphases. This will help the sermonizer adhere to biblical terminology as he collects, assimilates, and arranges the material for his sermon. The need for adhering to biblical terminology was forcefully set forth by William Ward Ayer.[9] The preacher might concentrate upon the study of a doctrine within a cluster of Bible books, within one Bible book, or within a segment of a Bible book. For example, he might study the doctrine of the Lord's return in 1 and 2 Thessalonians, or the doctrine of Christ in Colossians, or the doctrine of the Holy Spirit in Romans 8. Doctrines are set forth directly in these passages. Doctrines are often set forth indirectly in narrative portions.

The preacher's preaching program should reflect a coverage of the major and minor doctrines of scripture either directly or indirectly. Gerald J. Jud says that one of the ancient skills which must be updated is the pastor's ability to use biblical theology.[10] He must be an expert in it. The preacher will therefore find it helpful to group the doctrines of the Bible into two categories which he might label "major doctrines" and "minor doctrines." As he begins to study a Bible doctrine, he should collect the references to that doctrine. He may do this by tracing a doctrinal word directly in the Scriptures or by getting help from an analytical concordance or topical Bible. A survey of some books on Bible doctrine will also help him at this point. The following three books will provide an introductory survey of some of the major doctrines: *The Great Doctrines of the Bible* by William Evans, *In Understanding Be Men* by T. C. Hammond, and *Know What You Believe* by Paul E. Little.

As the references are located, they should be defined by comparing all Bible references and by using such extrabiblical helps as necessary. The doctrinal references should be related to the context of scripture where located and also to the total pattern of biblical truth. The doctrine should then be related to personal experience.

The preparation for preaching on a doctrine should include a survey of biblical and systematic theologies to discover the various headings which should be included in a discussion of the particular doctrine. One of these headings may give the preacher the theme or a point for his sermon.

### THE SERMONIC APPLICATION OF DOCTRINAL MATERIAL

Merril R. Abbey suggests that when preaching on doctrine we should make a double analysis both of the text and the audience.[11] The preacher should not only study his passage, but he should also study his people. He should be certain that doctrinal preaching will meet human needs. There are several inferences which might be drawn from such a declaration. One inference is that there are some doctrines better taught in a class than preached from the pulpit. Such doctrines are important but do not have direct bearing upon the day-by-day life of the individual. The second inference is that doctrinal preaching must include exposition plus application. It was Spurgeon who said that the sermon begins where the application begins. The good doctrine preacher should be proficient in applying doctrinal truth to daily living.

All else may be for nought if formulating a proper application is not uppermost in the preacher's mind. Since the lack of application has so often been noted as a weakness in doctrinal preaching, we proceed to examine this rhetorical function rather carefully. The importance of application is developed by Whitesell when he says:

> The selection of a text and the framing of a title have application in mind. The phrasing of the sermon thesis should point in the direction of application. The explanatory part of an expository sermon often has the elements of application in it. In making truth plain, the bearing of that truth on conduct is almost certain to be evident.[12]

To my knowledge, there is not one book in print devoted exclusively to a discussion of the functional element of sermonic application. One must find this material within general books on homiletic theory. Reu in his book *Homiletics* devotes twenty-five pages to the subject and Whitesell in his book *Power in Expository Preaching* devotes twelve pages.

Application is the rhetorical process by which truth is brought to bear directly upon individuals in order to persuade them.[13] Baird sees application as helping the audience see the relevance of the truth and what the truth has to do with them. It should also make clear what they ought to do about the truth. The application answers the question, "So what?"[14] Application is a moral or spiritual term denoting the use which is to be made of the sermon. The illustration is the picture or photograph that goes along with an abstract idea and serves to assist application. A discourse without application would be only a declamation. J. W. Etter puts it this way: "A preacher preaching a sermon without application would be like a physician giving to his patient a lecture on general health, and forgetting to write him a prescription."[15]

Application should be present in a sermon because many of those in the audience lack the spiritual, homiletical, hermeneutical, and mental skills necessary to apply the truth of the sermon to themselves. Many lack the will or desire to apply the truth of the sermon to sensitive areas in their lives.

Application not only clarifies the responsibility the individual must ascertain in the truth of the sermon but how that responsibility be fulfilled or carried out. Application shows how the goal of preaching—changed lives—may be accomplished.

Specific possibilities for effecting change should be enumerated in the sermon. In some cases, the average member of an audience has not given serious thought to the biblical truth being expounded and cannot readily assimilate the truth for himself. How the truth can be utilized by the hearer must then be clearly developed by the preacher. Randolph asserts that where concretion or application is lacking one does not merely find a poor sermon, but no sermon at all. The Bible itself intends for such preaching in which the claim of God is seen in the concrete context of the claims of men.[16]

Randolph substitutes the term *concretion* for what is commonly called application. He states that concretion is the process whereby the meaning of the biblical text is brought to expression in the situation of the hearers. Concretion stresses doing. Concretion is concerned with participation in what has been said as the hearer carries it forth into life, and "it is obviously of great importance to dynamic preaching which swings into revolution."[17]

Koller includes both application and illustration in what is referred to as the *six rhetorical processes*. These include: narration, interpretation, illustration, application, argumentation, and exhortation. In addition, Koller says, "The truth may often be more effectively applied to the hearer by implication than by direct statement. A well chosen illustration is often the most effective means."[18]

One function of illustration when used with the rhetorical

process of application is to arouse interest on the part of the hearer in the application of the sermon. During extended exposition or explanation the mind tends to wander or become tired. The important personal application of the sermon may be missed if the mind is not stirred to attention.

Illustrations will also make the application more concrete. The right kind of illustration provokes a mental picture in which the hearer actually sees the point of application. The truth and meaning of the application are thus delineated and clarified. The illustration aids concretion and facilitates the hearer in knowing what he is being called upon to do. Closely akin to this function of illustration is the substantial part that illustration had in impressing the application upon the mind of the hearer. People generally remember the illustrations in a sermon longer than any other of its elements.

Another use that illustration has is in making the application persuasive. The application must occur to the hearer as being significant in his Christian experience. The application is weak if it does not move the hearer to do something about it. Much of the persuasive power of any sermon and its application is found in its illustrations.

Illustrations also make the application practical. They bring the application down into common life and show how it can be applied amid the temptations, trials, drudgery, and complex relations of the hearer within society.

Briefly, an illustration awakens the hearer's interest and leads him to listen to the application. It helps to make the application clear. The impressions it helps to produce are remembered longer. The illustration exerts a force of proof which helps to persuade.

Few things weaken the application more than unnecessary words. Therefore caution in the use of illustrations is in order. Jones gives several guidelines to be kept in mind when using illustrations. Search until an apt illustration is found. Also, when quoting from any source, quote accurately. The preacher should avoid illustrations that require too much explaining and must exercise restraint in the number of illustrations used. In addition, never illustrate the obvious and always seek for variety in the illustrations used. Be sure the illustration is subordinate to the truth being preached. Finally, Jones says, "An illustration should be primarily structural rather than decorative. Never use an illustration . . . that attracts attention from the theme of the sermon."[19]

To these Whitesell adds that the preacher should use Bible illustrations freely. They are always appropriate and can be used over and over. The Holy Spirit will use them more readily than one may surmise. Old familiar illustrations must be used sparingly. The preacher should not apologize for using personal illustrations. If it is in its proper place there is no need to apologize for using it. If it is not in its proper place neither God nor man will excuse him for using it. Whitesell finds short illustrations are better than long ones. Furthermore, one must particularize and concretize the illustration as much as possible without unduly lengthening it. The preacher should tell the truth in illustrations and not put himself as part of the illustration unless it is a fact. He should acknowledge the source of an illustration if it is someone else's peculiar property. In addition, he should not tell stories about people in the audience. Finally, limiting humorous illustrations to a minimum in serious destiny-shaping biblical preaching is a point that should be emphasized.[20]

The preacher will generally position the application in the sermon outline in one of two ways. First he could use the *continued* or *running application* wherein truth is applied to the hearer at various intervals throughout the sermon. Secondly, he may choose to retain the application until the end of the sermon where it will form part of the conclusion. This is the *compact application*. Hervey points out that the chief excellences of many Puritan sermons were their continual applications. In his counsels to preachers, Hervey finds that in order to set forth the Word of God in a proper way and to advantage, two things are essential: a declaration of what is contained in the text, and an application of the same to the hearts and consciences of the audience.[21]

Porter supports the continued or running application with some reservation. Porter also cites Claude's essay as recommending some texts to be treated in the way of continued application. The main concern on Porter's part, however, is that the running application will not likely produce any single and strong impression on the hearers.[22] On the other hand, Pattison recommends the use of continuing application. He feels that always reserving the application for the conclusion will almost always surely make it stale and pointless. The application is then anticipated by the hearer, and comes when he is forearmed, forewarned, and on his guard, or when he is too tired to feel the force of the application. Far wiser is the preacher that carries a thread of application through the entire sermon.

While the application should not be kept until the close of the sermon, it is equally unfortunate to let the sermon die out with no application at all. Pattison recalls an old whaler's comment on his pastor's effort, "A nice sermon enough, but there was no harpoon in it."[23]

Sturtevant adds that in uniform application the whole discourse is to be precisely the same character as the concluding part of other sermons. It is in fact a peroration extended so as to occupy the whole time of the preacher. If judiciously introduced, it will gain and fix the hearer's attenion and, if skillfully managed, will retain it to the end.[24]

In recent years the continued application is in wider use than the practice of leaving the application for the conclusion. Application is drawn usually after the discussion of each main division in the sermon as well as at the close. This was what prompted Jeff Brown to say that each division of the sermon should contain a conclusion.[25] This could be called a *divisional application*.

The application in a sermon must be personal, but it must also include means and methods. How to do it must always follow the exhortation to do it. This may well be the weakest point in most preaching. The application, then, should deal with particulars. Developing a specific application, employing the application, and audience response to the application must now be considered.

According to Coffin, most sermons fail because the preacher has not made plain to himself precisely what he is seeking to press the hearers to be and to do.[26] At the outset, the preacher must determine the focus of the application. The preacher should decide exactly who is to receive the thrust of the application. He should aim the sermon at the largest number possible.[27]

In an effort to personalize and localize, the preacher will have more success if the material of the application is aimed at specific individuals in the audience, rather than at a mythical person composing the characteristics of various members of the audience. If the preacher selects materials that apply causually to every member in the audience he will run the risk of choosing items that fit no one exactly and therefore do not move the hearers to a response. Farmer follows with a similar observation when he says, "I have sometimes found it a help to write with a definite person in a definite situation before my mind's eye, putting to myself such questions as these: How would this sound to him? Would he understand it? Would it seem any other than an airy and irrelevant abstraction?"[28]

During the course of preparation it will also be helpful if the preacher frequently sees himself as the hearer. Would this consideration move him if he were the hearer? Would this argument avail in his case? Does he receive help and comfort here? Would he himself do that which he is counseling others to do? Breed comments that the preacher must remember that the measure of his success in preaching is to be found alone in the degree in which the application of the sermon is observed and practiced by the audience. Not brilliant rhetoric, sound argument, or telling illustrations, but one's positive usefulness is the measure of one's success.[29] Lewis becomes even more practical and specific. Some ministers, Lewis finds, sharpen their audience awareness by keeping a card on their desks with the names of six or as many as twelve parishioners on it. For example, the names of a six-year-old boy, a fourteen-year-old girl, a teenage couple, a young married couple, parents of a young family, a business man, a widow, and a retired couple. By preparing a sermon to help these specific people the entire audience finds something vital in the message.[30] It should also be remembered that the preacher must never single out a person by name or give details so that an audience can determine the hearer to which the preacher is referring.

For Breed, the application is found both in the preacher and in the text. The application in the preacher resides in his spirit and manner rather than in any language which he employs to express it. It will be conveyed by his sincerity, earnestness, and fidelity to the Word of God. A preacher must guard against detached preaching. This consists in handing over a course of thought to an audience with permission to take it or leave it upon its own merits. It is as though the preacher does not want the audience to be influenced by him but merely to consider whether the message is true and good, and to decide for themselves what to do with it. The preacher must be the embodiment of the truth which he announces and it must have a vital power. One mistake that a preacher can make is thinking that truth contains its own force. The application is also in the text. The text is chosen because the preacher sees the application in it, and the subject of the text is so announced by the preacher that it contains the application in its initial form. Proper handling of the text can bring out the correct application whereas improper handling may obscure the obvious application.[31]

The application dare not be anything alien to and imported into the text, as though the preacher needed to add to the contents of the text something of his own. He must, on the contrary, take the Word of God, whose meaning in the past he has ascertained, and set it unaltered and unabridged in the midst of the present. He must let it say to men of today what it said to men of the past. To make sound and forceful application, Whitesell says,

> Truth must be lifted out of its local and temporary references and shown to be timeless and universal. There is something powerful about elemental, eternal truth. Such truth lies underneath the surface of all Biblical material. One of the major tasks of preaching is to find and lay bare these timeless truths in such a way that they will challenge and move the listeners. These truths are essential to good sermon titles, theses, main points, and application. The normal mind has capacity to see and recognize at once the force of timeless truth. To apply such truth is relatively easy, for it almost applies itself.[32]

The timeless truth, once discovered in the text, must be set forth in all naturalness so that the application will grow by an inner necessity out of the text and will be nothing else than the organic unfolding of the text. The main thought in the text will be the main thought in the application. What is subordinate in the text will be subordinate in the application. What is not found in the text will not be found in the application. Reu summarizes by saying,

> The whole application of the Word of God to the present day must follow the lines and reproduce the characteristic features of the text, so that the text may without difficulty be recognized from the application. This is demanded by the dignity of the text as well as by the homiletic conscience of the preacher. The homilete must so completely assimilate this principle that it will become his second nature, and that he will be unable to act contrary to it because his conscience will not permit.[33]

Before the application can live and move in the souls of the hearers it must burn and glow in the heart of the preacher. Therefore, the preacher should write out the application to be used in the sermon so he may develop clarity of thought and pointedness of direction and focus. Writing aids in expressing briefly, accurately, and pointedly what otherwise is likely to be profuse, vague, and loosely stated. Jones quotes Bacon as saying, "Conversation makes a ready man, reading makes a full man, and writing makes an exact man."[34] Writing also compels greater completeness of preparation.

As a general rule, application is made in connection with each spiritual truth discussed. There are times, however, when it would be well to make application at the close of each subdivision or at the end of each main division. Only a brief summary line from this paragraph will appear on the outline to be taken to the pulpit. However, the careful preparation behind that summary line will give the application force and comprehensiveness during delivery. Sangster proposes that any preacher should hang up the word *how* over his desk to remind himself that sermon preparation is not complete until this task is done.

The clarity and force of the application paragraph can be

improved if the following are kept in mind during preparation: Is it clear? Is it interesting and significant? Is it vivid? Is it convincing? Also, the language of application depends upon nouns and pronouns for its effectiveness. First person and second person pronouns make application direct and personal. It was James Denney who wrote, "The man who shoots above the target does not thereby prove that he has superior ammunition. He simply proves that he is not an accurate shot."[35] Ian MacPherson quotes Boswell as saying of Johnson that in the cut and thrust of debate Johnson wasted no time in brandishing his sword but "was through your body in an instant."[36] Applications which have to be labored for too long a time and illustrations which must be explained are less than the best.

Doctrinal preaching is needed in our day just as it has been needed in past days. The emphasis should be placed upon biblical doctrine. It would seem that the two best sermon patterns for doctrinal preaching would be the modification and clarification type three. If doctrinal preaching is to be appreciated by our people we must make effective use of illustrations and make certain that the doctrinal truths are shown to be practical for salvation and edification. Doctrinal preaching involves the teaching of doctrine plus its application to daily living. Power comes to preaching when we herald the great declarations of biblical truth related to God and man. This is doctrinal preaching.

## Reading List

Abbey, Merril R. *Living Doctrines in a Vital Pulpit*. Nashville: Abingdon, 1965.

Baird, John Edward. *Preparing for Platform and Pulpit*. Nashville: Abingdon, 1968.

Blackwood, Andrew W. *Doctrinal Preaching for Today*. New York: Abingdon-Cokesbury, 1956.

Braga, James. *How to Prepare Bible Messages*. Portland, Oreg.: Multnomah, 1969.

Brastow, Lewis Orsmond. *The Work of the Preacher*. Boston: Pilgrim, 1914.

Breed, David Riddle. *Preparing to Preach*. New York: Hodder & Stoughton, 1911.

Brooks, Phillips. *Yale Lecture on Preaching.* New York: Dutton, 1879.

Brown, Jeff. *A Handbook for the Preacher at Work.* Grand Rapids: Baker, 1958.

Coffin, Henry S. *Communion Through Preaching.* New York: Scribner, 1952.

Cox, Harvey. *The Secular City.* New York: Macmillan, 1966.

Dabney, Robert L. *Sacred Rhetoric: Lectures on Preaching.* New York: Randolph, 1870.

Etter, John W. *The Preacher and His Sermon.* Dayton, Ohio: United Brethren, 1883.

Evans, William. *The Great Doctrines of the Bible.* Chicago: Moody, 1949.

Farmer, Herbert H. *The Servant of the Word.* New York: Scribner, 1942.

Hammond, T. C. *In Understanding Be Men.* Chicago: Inter-Varsity, n.d.

Johnson, Herrick. *The Ideal Ministry.* New York: Revell, 1913.

Jones, Ilion T. *Principles and Practice of Preaching.* New York: Abingdon, 1956.

Jordan, Gerald Ray. *You Can Preach.* New York: Revell, 1951.

Jud, Gerald J. *Crisis in the Church.* Philadelphia: Pilgrim, 1968.

Koller, Charles W. *Expository Preaching Without Notes.* Grand Rapids: Baker, 1962.

Lewis, Ralph L. *Speech for Persuasive Preaching.* Berne, Ind.: Economy, 1968.

Little, Paul E. *Know What You Believe.* Wheaton, Ill.: Scripture Press, 1970.

MacPherson, Ian. *The Art of Illustrating Sermons.* New York: Abingdon, 1964.

McCracken, Robert J. *The Making of the Sermon.* New York: Harper, 1956.

Pattison, T. Harwood. *The Making of the Sermon.* Philadelphia: Amer. Bapt., 1898.

Phelps, Austin. *The Theory of Preaching.* London: Dickinson, 1882.

Porter, Ebenezer. *Lectures on Homiletics and Preaching, and on Public Prayer.* Andover, New York: Flagg, Gould, & Newman, 1834.

Randolph, David James. *The Renewal of Preaching.* Philadelphia: Fortress, 1969.

Reid, Clyde. *The Empty Pulpit.* New York: Harper & Row, 1967.

Reu, M. *Homiletics.* Chicago: Wartburg, 1922.

Richardson, Alan. *Christian Apologetics.* New York: Harper, 1947.

Rock, A. *Unless They Be Sent.* Dubuque, Iowa: Brown, 1953.

Schenck, Ferdinand Schureman. *Modern Practical Theology.* New York: Funk & Wagnalls, 1903.

Skinner, Thomas Harvey. *Aids to Revealing and Hearing.* New York: Taylor, 1839.

Stevenson, Dwight. *In the Biblical Preacher's Workshop.* Nashville: Abingdon, 1967.

Sturtevant, S. *The Preacher's Manual.* New York: Riker, 1840.

von Allmen, Jean Jacques. *Preaching and Congregation.* Richmond: John Knox, 1962.

Whitesell, Faris D. *Power in Expository Preaching.* Westwood, N.J.: Revell, 1963.

————. *The Art of Preaching.* Grand Rapids: Zondervan, 1950.

# 7

## Biblical Preaching
## and Evangelization

> When they therefore were come together, they asked of him, say-
> ing, Lord, wilt thou at this time restore again the kingdom to
> Israel? And he said unto them, It is not for you to know the times
> or the seasons, which the Father hath put in his own power. But
> ye shall receive power, after that the Holy Ghost is come upon
> you: and ye shall be witnesses unto me both in Jerusalem, and in
> all Judaea, and in Samaria, and unto the uttermost part of the
> earth. And when he had said these things, while they beheld, he
> was taken up; and a cloud received him out of their sight. And
> while they looked steadfastly into heaven as he went up, behold,
> two men stood by them in white apparel; which also said, Ye men
> of Galilee, why stand ye gazing into heaven? This same Jesus,
> which is taken up from you into heaven, shall so come in like
> manner as ye have seen him go into heaven (Ac 1:6-11).

IT HAS BEEN SAID that the world is growing pagan at the rate
of 38 million souls a year. Only 3 percent of the lost ever
attend church. Only 5 percent of those who come to Christ
come without a personal invitation. In 1850, it took five
Christians to lead one soul to Christ. It now takes an average
of 1,000 laymen and six pastors to lead one soul to Christ in
365 days. Eighty percent of those who will be saved will be
younger than 25 years. Seventy-five percent of our Sunday
school students leave the Sunday school by the time they are
18 years of age. We have 400 million more in the world today
without the gospel than we had thirty years ago. Billy Graham
stated at the World Congress of Evangelism that the population
was increasing at the rate of 40 million people a year. This
would mean that 110,000 people a day, or 4,500 an hour, or 75

every minute would have to be won to Christ just to keep up
with the population increase. We dare not just stand here. We
must do something.

We face a different world today than the early church faced.
The world of that day was unfamiliar with the gospel. America
is saturated with it. The first century had no neat company
of professing Christians against which to measure the gospel.
We have such today and unfortunately this sometimes hurts
evangelism more than helps it. There was no history of evangelism to overcome. The saints were not biased against certain
forms and practices of evangelism. There were no organized
programs to be maintained so that evangelism had to be inserted where there was a break in the program. They lacked
the equipment and gadgets which today are sometimes more
of a bane than a blessing. There were no institutional by-
products to hinder the work such as high pressure fund raising
enterprises. Best of all, they were living in the afterglow of
Christ's ministry on earth. Our situation certainly differs from
that of the early church.

The present-day church appears to be having transmission
trouble. It appears to be confused in regarding itself more as
a reservoir than as a channel. Our churches lack numbers, but
our prisons are full. Our minds are enlightened, but our morals
are decadent. We have built big churches, but they have become
monuments. The people are asking, "What mean these stones?"
At one time we wanted to be involved in a movement, but now
find that instead we are shackled with the indebtedness of a
monument. We must shift our emphasis from building an institution to that of changing the world for the glory of God. It
appears that we have been doing a thousand good but secondary things that the Lord never told us to do. We have been
majoring in minors and specializing in the trivial, while millions
have been left to populate hell. We need to remember that our
work is not sociology, but salvation. Our concern should not
be first of all reform, but redemption. It is not progress, but
pardon. It is not first of all culture, but conversion. It is not
economics, but evangelism.

A. C. Gettys, professor of religious education at Baylor College, defined evangelism as follows: "Evangelism means telling, teaching, or proclaiming the evangel, the 'Good News,' of the Christian religion in such a way that people will understand, accept, and live the message."[1] This message of God and from God was a part of the work of men both in the Old Testament and in the New Testament.

"Evangelism is that art of allowing oneself to be used as a channel by which the Holy Spirit may communicate Himself to others."[2] This personal desire, accompanied with the Word of God, is needed to get the heartbeat of God to heartbroken and sinful men.

Evangelism grows out of revival. Someone has said, "When the saints of God get on fire, then the sinners will come to see them 'burn.' " A study of revivals of the past reveals that their appeal was to the individual. We have replaced the individual today with a Social Security number. He can get lost in society. He can get lost in school, and unfortunately he can get lost in church. In revivals there was an emphasis upon piety. Conditional separation has never been a stepping stone toward revival. The preaching was doctrinal. Someone has suggested that we have congregations of doctrinal illiterates in our churches. If this be true, then maybe this is one reason that revival tarries. Revivals stress man's guilt and need for cleansing from sin. The cry of the psalmist poured out of the soul; "Search me, O God, and know my heart: try me, and know my thoughts: and see if there be any wicked way in me, And lead me in the way everlasting" (Ps 139:23-24). There was an emphasis upon human responsibility and personal duty: prayer, Bible study and visitation were emphasized.

As revival fires begin to burn there will come an intensity of feeling in the presentation of the preacher. Quintilian's maxim, "The speaker must be on fire who is anxious to reach the people," will become an actuality. It is this sacred fire which in the words of George MacDonald "breaks down every stockade of prejudice, every wall of stupidity and every rampart of indifference." It was this type of presentation which prompted one to say of the preaching of Thomas Chalmers, that he "buried his hearers under mountains of burning lava."

### REQUIREMENTS OF AN EVANGELISTIC PREACHER

At this point it may be well for us to consider a few of the basic requirements of one who feels called under God to proclaim the good news of Christ from the pulpit with the goal of helping one come to know Christ as Saviour. There should first of all be *preparation of mind and heart*. The preparation of mind may well include the memorization of the Scriptures so verses will be available at the bidding of the Spirit. The preparation of heart should include not only a cleansing from sin realizing that "If I regard iniquity in my heart, God will not hear me" (Ps 66:18), but also a manifestation of love toward others.

The second requirement is *passion*. It was John Watson who said, "Every movement which has stirred the depth of life and changed the face of history has sprung from some personal sentiment and powerful emotion." The world would rob us of the inflammatory touch of a Jeremiah or Isaiah. It would put in its place a cold bath of formalism and a creed of mental crystals. When Henry Martyn landed on India's shores for a short ten year ministry as his body was racked by illness, he is reported to have said, "Now let me burn out for Christ." This type of passion is needed in the pulpit evangelist.

The next requirement is that of *persistence*. Insurance companies, through surveys, have discovered that they do 80 percent of their business after making the fifteenth call on the prospect. We need to "compel them to come in" (Lk 14:23).

*Spiritual power* is the next requirement. It is the Holy Spirit who regenerates (Jn 3:3). It is the Holy Spirit who convicts (Jn 16:7-8). It is the Holy Spirit who seals (Eph 4:30). Without Him we can do nothing.

The ability to *plead* with the lost is necessary. The late Clarence McCartney said that *come* is God's favorite word. "The Spirit and the bride say, Come. And let him that heareth say, Come. And let him that is athirst come. And whosoever will, let him take the water of life freely" (Rev 22:17).

It was the combination of these qualities which spurred George Whitefield to ride 100,000 miles on horseback to share the Saviour. These also motivated Wesley throughout his life. At eighty-eight years of age he based his final sermon on the text, "Seek ye the LORD while he may be found" (Is 55:6).

To these marks of an evangelist, Graves says, "The preacher of the Gospel by virtue of his office is evangelical."[3] He is also evangelistic. His primary requisite is what Shedd calls "a heart glowing and beating with evangelical affections."[4]

Kern adds that the evangelist in his preaching should let nothing discourage him.[5] He should remain cheerful, hopeful, and sweet-spirited throughout. There should be no irritation of feeling when disappointed in the result of his efforts. This should only encourage him to be all the more earnest and indomitable.

Brastow states that it is a serious mistake for a minister to spend time in pursuits that are secondary in importance to him as a minister and to neglect his message.[6] It is his first duty to learn to handle the gospel of Christ effectively. It is important for this type of preaching that the preacher cultivate his feelings and affections. It is further of importance for him to cultivate his powers of imagination. Moral earnestness is also of central significance, and he should cultivate a strong and positive faith. This type of preaching demands a deep religious life on the part of the preacher. The evangelistic spirit should be cultivated.

Burrell states that our business is before and above all to bring the converted to Christ.[7] Hence every sermon should be evangelistic. There is no homiletic standpoint but Calvary.

## EVANGELISTIC PREACHING AND THE OLD TESTAMENT

The work of evangelism and evangelistic preaching is often thought of as part of serving God since Christ's coming and New Testament times. Certainly in its narrow sense and strictest definition this is true; but, in looking at the Bible and its message of God, we will see that there was a work of evangelism and evangelistic preaching in the Old Testament as well as in the New.

In the Old Testament it was a cry of God's prophets to the people to get right with God, to put away idols, to return to God. We could say that in the Old Testament the work of "revival" and a "call to revival" would be used closely in the work of evangelism.

C. E. Autrey, director of evangelism of the Southern Baptists, states,

> Revival is an instrument of evangelism. Evangelism is a far broader term. Evangelism is confronting the unregenerate with the doctrine of salvation. In the Old Testament, evangelism is confined to revival. There is little or no effort seen in the Old Testament to reach the nations for God. Revival is any special spiritual stirring which turns the people back to God. Often in the Old Testament these revival efforts would last a day or a week, but the effects would endure for a generation.[8]

Not only does the Old Testament provide evangelism through commands of God's prophets and servants, and through the atonement plan God offered from the very beginning to Adam and Eve when they sinned against Him, but we find passage after passage recorded which gives the basis for witnessing and preaching an evangelistic message. We will cite only a few of the many.

The Psalmist offers many passages for evangelistic preaching from his own personal encounters with God. In Psalm 85, we read, "Turn us, O God of our salvation, and cause thine anger toward us to cease" (v. 4), and "Wilt thou not revive us again: that thy people may rejoice in thee?" (v. 6). Horace Dean, president of the Christ for America evangelistic movement, referred to this passage in a plea for personal revival in the hearts of Christians.[9]

In pressing further for the personal revival in the hearts of Christians, Dean referred to Psalm 51 where, after David's dreadful sin, he turned to God in distress.

> This man of God cried to the Lord for a clean heart and a right spirit within. He could never be satisfied until he is restored to the fellowship which he once knew. After David is restored, he expects—and it is always true—that the restored child of God walking in the light, will be the means of winning others.[10]

In presenting patterns of prayer for evangelism and revival campaigns and services, the Old Testament provides a storehouse of references. Ezra was used of God to bring about a great revival as he prayed for God to bring a spiritual awakening

(Ezra 9-10). The greatest revival of the Old Testament was the movement under Hezekiah which transformed the whole nation of Judah from a state of lethargy and open rebellion against God, to where they sought forgiveness and the face of God in a new way (2 Ch 29-31).

Should the Old Testament have a place in evangelism and evangelistic preaching? Rather than ask the question, we should ask why it should not!

To find the pattern, the plan, and certainly the plea for evangelism and evangelistic preaching, we turn to the Old Testament and find that it is definitely there. And, it is there because evangelism is more than the work of men who want to hold a protracted meeting in a certain place. It is the work of God Himself. It is more than the New Testament for it is the message of the entire Bible.

## The Evangelistic Sermon

Breed advises that the evangelistic sermon must be exceedingly simple. The evangelist should cultivate a variety of forms for evangelistic sermons. It is of doubtful wisdom in preaching evangelistic sermons to address them directly to the uncovered. They should be presented to all classes and should include the entire congregation. Some will be aroused; some will be converted; but all will be helped, stimulated, and comforted. Evangelistic sermons should not always be preached at certain services. They should form a large part of a pastor's preaching work, since, in many cases, he should be his own evangelist. The evangelistic sermon is one which seeks to promote the conviction of sin and to lead a man to an immediate decision for Jesus Christ. The evangelistic sermon should be addressed to the conscience and should be positively instructive.[11]

The evangelistic sermon brings the hearer face to face with Christ as the Son of God and moves him to accept Him as Saviour and Lord. At certain seasons of the year, the evangelistic sermon can make its appeal with special force. In fact, the period between Thanksgiving and Easter may well become the harvest season of the Christian year.

Blackwood also writes about the characteristics of evangelistic preaching. He says that the source of material should be chiefly scriptural, and that the form of the message should be doctrinal, at least indirectly. Then, the style of the message is discussed. He stresses seven points in what he calls the style of the evangelistic sermon:

1. It should appeal to ordinary people.
2. It should be concrete, not abstract.
3. It should be notable for human interest.
4. The style of the soul-winning sermon is simple.
5. Evangelistic preaching is personal.
6. Evangelistic preaching is direct.
7. Evangelistic preaching is urgent.[12]

Ozora S. Davis adds the following marks of the evangelistic sermon. The evangelistic sermon is directed accurately at the hearer and at life as it is being lived now. The evangelistic sermon must be directed to the whole hearer. That is, it must seek to convince his mind, to move his feelings, and persuade his will to the point where it registers a new decision concerning the dominant motives of his life. An evangelistic sermon needs to be grounded in the soundest logic and to be of such a character that it will bear searching debate. The evangelistic sermon must be warmed and bathed in the passion with which the preacher believes.[13] The most important factor, however, in the evangelistic sermon is the direct drive for a decision in favor of the message on the part of the hearers. The evangelistic sermon must be simply keyed to the note of invitation and persuasion.[14] Some additional characterizing features of evangelistic preaching are noted by Herrick Johnson:

1. The sermon that is after a soul has no tomorrow in it. Its accepted time is now.
2. The sermon that is after a soul, is not a bow "drawn at a venture."
3. The sermon that is after a soul will, therefore, have a singleness of aim, knowledge of the actual human nature aimed at, all possible study of that soul's individuality, and an individuality in the sermon answering to the individuality of the man.

4. The sermon that is after a soul, like the Master, is "filled with compassion."[15]

V. L. Stanfield adds these characteristics of effective evangelistic preaching:

1. The evangelistic sermon should be biblical in content.
2. The evangelistic sermon should be positive. Much gospel preaching has been "bad news" rather than "good news." The gospel is good news of what God has done, is doing, and can do in and through Jesus Christ.
3. Evangelistic preaching should be comparatively brief.
4. An evangelistic sermon should be marked by a sense of urgency.
5. An evangelistic sermon should have the mark of authority.

To my knowledge, Stanfield is one of the few who writes on the construction of an evangelistic sermon. He mentions the body of the evangelistic sermon.

First, the outline should be easy to follow. . . . This means that it should be simply stated . . . it should be logical. Make the outline easy to grasp.

Second, the body of the sermon should be orderly. . . . [and] have a careful plan.

Third, the body of the sermon should adequately develop the subject. . . . The ultimate aim of the evangelistic sermon is commitment.

Stanfield goes on to speak of the introduction of an evangelistic sermon. He states that

It should endeavor to capture attention. . . . The preacher . . . may do this with humor; he may do it with common interest material; he may do it with current events.

The introduction should be fairly brief.

The evangelistic sermon introduction should be marked by assurance. The preacher should not be hesitant; he should never apologize.

The conclusion is discussed by Stanfield along the following major points: (1) it shoud be appropriate, (2) the conclusion should also be direct, and (3) a sermon conclusion should be marked by strength or intensity. Intensity does not mean loudness; some of the most intense sermon conclusions are quiet.[16]

Brastow says that there are certain additional homiletical qualities which are especially useful in this type of preaching. The introduction will be specifically solicitous to win and fix attention at the outset. The conclusion is naturally shorter, more compact, and more concentrated in form than that of the didactic sermon. The cultivation of good perspective, of balance of parts, and economy of force is another important interest. One needs to know not only what to say, but how much and when, and where and how to stop.[17]

The presentation of evangelistic preaching is discussed by Menzies who adds that the evangelistic gospel must be presented picturesquely and with intellectual force.[18]

Several additional factors in the delivery of the evangelistic sermon are stressed by Stanfield. First, it should be marked by zeal or enthusiasm. When the preacher realizes that the destiny of the human soul is at stake, he cannot speak flippantly. The concern in his heart should show in his delivery. A preacher should speak quietly until his inner feelings demand that he speak enthusiastically. Secondly, he says that the evangelistic sermon should be noted for freedom of delivery. Finally, above all other preaching, evangelistic preaching must be completely dependent upon the Holy Spirit.[19]

## MOTIVATION AND EVANGELISTIC PREACHING

There is a variety of motives which bring men to Christ. Hoyt suggests five.

1. Some men begin the Christian life under a sense of duty.
2. The appeal to moral imagination, especially youth.
3. The mystical elements of the gospel make the strongest appeal. Christ as the revelation of God and the giver of life is certainly a strong appeal.
4. Appeal to a sense of shame over moral failure.
5. Appeal to fear.[20]

Brastow discusses six different motives: the intellectual motive, the aesthetic motive, the paracletic motive, the emotional motive, the moral motive, and the social motive.[21] Two or three of the motives listed should be clarified as to meaning. The paracletic motive refers to that situation where sorrows, disappointments, hardships, and dissatifactions of life prepare many for the reception of Christ as the One who brings comfort, strength, and peace. The appeal to fear is involved in the emotional motive. The moral motive involves working directly on the results of the early training of the conscience.

R. W. Dale adds to the list of motives which bring men to Christ. He says that some men are drawn to God by the hope of escaping from a vague dissatisfaction with themselves and with the poverty of their lives. There are some again, who begin to think of God through the shame and self-disgust which are the result of moral failure and the discovery of moral weakness. Others, whose moral life is generous and aspiring, may approach Christ through ethical precepts of His which require perfection of the kind that is altogether impossible apart from the power of the Holy Spirit. There are many who are drawn to Christ by His life—drawn to Him, not because they are conscious either of moral weakness which His life is eager to strengthen, or of sin which His love is willing to forgive, or of unintelligible cravings which His love is able to satisfy—but by His love itself.[22]

Some methods of motivation are considered by Stanfield. There are four methods which he lists:

1. The use of certain basic evangelistic appeals
2. The appeal to basic drives
3. Usage of the principles of persuasion
4. The use of an epitome, example, or illustration[23]

These methods require some explanation. First consider motivation through the use of basic evangelistic appeals. There are nine evangelistic appeals: (1) deliverance from sin; (2) an innate hunger for God; (3) the best way of life; (4) the resources of life; (5) the best use of influences; (6) the almost innate desire for the better—better community, better home, better church; (7) the response to sacrifice; (8) the answer to life after death; and finally (9) the appeal to fear. Henry Sloane Coffin and George E. Sweazy discuss and advocate the use of this last appeal. Sweazy lists twenty-one evangelistic appeals and emphasizes the importance of such appeals by stating that the only assumption the evangelist can make is that God has provided some way to approach every human being. When one way fails, he must try another. The person who has been awakened to the need for just one small part of Christianity is likely to begin to appreciate the rest of it.

Another method of motivation is the use of basic drives. The first one is *self-preservation.* You can promise the individual eternal life, life in Christ which begins now and continues without end. Another basic drive is for *personal happiness.* Other basic drives are for *recognition* or *prestige, security, freedom, adventure,* and *satisfaction.* In Christ there is freedom from sin and freedom from anxiety. In Him there is the satisfying fact of life to know that your sins are forgiven and that you are reconciled to God.

### INVITATIONS AND EVANGELISTIC PREACHING

There are several aspects of invitation in evangelistic preaching. First of all, we should discuss the reasons for using invitations. Whitesell gives us four reasons: invitations are biblical, logical, psychological, and practical.[24]

Autrey points out several additional reasons for giving an invitation:

1. The danger of otherwise frustrating those who hear the preacher preach for a verdict without providing an opportunity for commitment. Commitment is the purpose of the invitation.

2. The invitation should be given to complete the gospel message. The invitation is the climax of the sermon.

3. Give the invitation to get decision. The difference between success and failure in evangelism often lies just here.

4. The invitation is historical. Through the succeeding centuries representatives of Christ have in one form or another bibli-

cally urged men to respond to the gospel. Those who preach for a verdict also call for a decision.[25]

Two more reasons for giving invitations are mentioned by Stanfield:

1. To give invitations is natural. When you preach a gospel sermon . . . of the grace of God and the love of God, it is just natural to say, "He did this for you! Will you believe it?" To give an invitation is inherent in the gospel.
2. To give an invitation is essential. It is essential for the people. They are without God and without hope. When they hear this message of reconciliation, they need to be invited to receive it. It is also essential for the preacher. He needs to complete his sermon and lay claim upon the congregation.[26]

Second, the method of giving the invitation should be considered. Sweazey gives us seven suggestions for giving an invitation:

1. Naturally, with no forced imitation of another's manner. The minister must learn by steps, going only as far each time as he can go without feeling awkward.
2. Firmly, with no fumbling of timidity.
3. Confidently, as though expecting a response.
4. Clearly, telling exactly what the decision means and how it is to be expressed.
5. Gently, not with high pressure or dominating methods.
6. Friendly, not oratorically.
7. Earnestly, as a solemn and holy matter—not as an unimportant item in the service.[27]

Whitesell suggests sixty-five ways to give the invitation, of which we list sixteen: clearly, confidently, earnestly, courteously, honestly, optimistically, naturally, prayerfully, positively, encouragingly, thoroughly, and in entire dependence upon the Holy Spirit, resourcefully, vigorously, scripturally, and compassionately.[28]

Autrey also offers some suggestions which contain a few fundamental principles regarding the invitation.

1. The preacher must bring himself to the proper frame of mind. It must begin in the heart of the evangelist. He must

be gravely concerned for the lost in the audience. He must come to this concern and poise through much prayer. He should begin praying for the invitation period the day before it is given. Let him pray until his greatest desire is to see the lost saved.

2. Plan the invitation. The invitation must be as carefully planned as the body of the sermon.

3. Give the invitation with poise. This is the time to be tender, sweet, persuasive, yet firm.

4. Give the invitation courteously. The soul-winner must respect the rights of others, even the right to die in their sins if they persist. It never pays to embarrass others. A preacher should be as courteous in the sacred pulpit as he is in the home of his host.

5. Give the invitation clearly. Make the plan of salvation plain. Make each proposition plain. Speak the language of the people. When men understand clearly what is said, only then can the truth be effective.

6. Depend at all times on the Holy Spirit. The Holy Spirit is more concerned about the results of any given service than any Christian could ever be.

7. Extend the invitation the proper length of time. Do not stop too soon. Let the invitation run as long as folk are moving and the Spirit is working.[29]

We should consider briefly the kinds of invitations that can be given. There are four primary types: (1) the invitation to the lost to receive Christ as Lord and Saviour, (2) the invitation to Christians for rededication, (3) the invitation to transfer membership, (4) the invitation or call to Christian service. The vital place of the Holy Spirit should be given special mention. Autrey makes reference to it when he says:

1. All involved will rely on the Holy Spirit for guidance and power. Two things guarantee a successful evangelistic service; namely, prospects in earnest and the power of the Holy Spirit.

2. Give Him a chance to work. God is a jealous God and will not share His glory with any man. All human instruments must get out of the way or be completely surrendered as tools in God's hands.

3. Give Him credit.[30]

### Types of Evangelistic Preaching

Many writers in this field do not think that there is a unique "type" of evangelistic preaching. However, Edgar Whitaker Work points out that there are five types of evangelistic preaching:

1. The particular type of which is the illustrative, narrative kind, dealing mainly with life and its experiences. It proceeds mainly by exhortation.
2. The teaching form of evangelism. Here the force of evangelism and the force of the sermon rests mainly upon fact, history and information.
3. The personal type. The appeal is usually to realities and needs that are all too apparent in personality and life.
4. The scriptural type, where the power of the sermon is that of a text or passage of the Bible made vital and intense in the experience of the soul—deep answering unto deep.
5. The doctrinal type, where the influence of the sermon consists for the most part in the explanation and enforcement of Christian teaching.[31]

There are several methods which might be used to classify evangelistic sermons. One of these is in terms of sermon structure.[32] If a preacher desired to survey a subject connected with salvation, he might use what Blackwood and Mark have referred to as the *adverbial* or *interrogative sermon*. An interrogative adverb or pronoun forms the basis of each main point. The *couplet* sermon has been suggested by Mark. This sermon structure is composed of two related parts. It is basically a textual message. This type of sermon might be used for example when preaching on Romans 10:9. The *inferential, deductive,* or *implicational* sermon is based upon inferences drawn from the verse which relates to the subject of the verse. In Isaiah 53:6, there are implications of the extent, manner, motive, and result of human waywardness (see Sample Sermon Outline 4 in chapter 3). Mark suggests an *objections-answered* sermon. Each main point would consist of an objection which the listener might raise which he could use as an excuse or reason for not following the basic recommendation of the sermon. If the preacher were preaching on Isaiah 55:6-7, the listener might be prompted to pose certain objections which the sermonizer should in turn answer. One homiletician has suggested the *practical* sermon. This is structured so that each main point is a distinct application of the truth of the text. (This type of sermon is referred to in chapter 3 under the heading of clarification type 3.) Jones suggested a *question* sermon in which each main point is in the form of a question. A sermonizer might be dealing with the question, "How can a man be justified?" (Job 25:4). He might proceed to ask, Can a man be justified by works of morality? (Ro 4:5-8). Can a man be justified by rites of religion? (Ro 4:9-12). Can a man be justified by deeds of the law? (Ro 4:13-25). The answer to each question would be no. The preacher could then use a positive conclusion showing that man can be justified by grace (Ro 3:24), by blood (Ro 3:25), and by faith (Ro 3:28). The *symphonic* sermon suggested by Caldwell and Stidger repeats a phrase, sentence, or couplet throughout the sermon in order that it might be impressed upon the minds of the listeners. "Ye must be born again" (Jn 3:7) might be such a sentence.

Evangelistic sermons might be classified in terms of the subject matter.[33] A *beatitude* such as Psalm 32:1-2 might be used as a basis for a sermon. A *biography* of scripture such as that of Andrew (Jn 1, 6, 12) would provide homiletical possibilities. There are several *commandments* as Mark 10:21 which provide a challenge for evangelism. *Conversations* of the Bible such as the one carried on between Nicodemus and Jesus provide preaching potential. There are many accounts of *conversions* such as that of the eunuch in Acts 8 which would provide an example of evangelism in action. Doctrinal preaching has been associated with evangelism through the years. The creed of the criminal in Luke 23:39-43 could combine the two areas of doctrine and evangelism. There are many *questions* of the Bible which provide preaching possibilities such as the one asked by Pilate, "What then shall I do with Jesus who is called the Christ?"

The sermonizer might classify evangelistic sermons in terms of the size of the portion of scripture used as a basis for the sermon.[34] The *book* of 1 John provides the answer to the question, How can I know that I am saved? The fourth *chapter* of

John's gospel shows us that a revelation of a possible satisfaction (4:14), personal sin (4:16-17), and a present Saviour (4:26) can be used by the Spirit of God for the transformation of a life. The first *paragraph* of 1 John 3 emphasizes the family name, life, and hope of one who belongs to God. A single *verse,* such as Luke 19:5, has preaching possibilities, as Zachaeus realized that Jesus knew where he was, who he was, needed him, and wanted him. These relationships and realizations prompted him to "get off the limb" and seek the Saviour. Even a single word such as *forgiven* has great possibilities for evangelistic preaching (see Sample Sermon Outline 2 in chapter 3).

### EVANGELISTS AND EVANGELISTIC SERMONS

In order to improve one's own evangelistic preaching, one might study the lives and sermons of the following preachers. In the Patristic Age, he would want to consider the preaching of *John Chrysostom* who is referred to by Dargan as one of the greatest preachers of all time. He would also want to study the preaching of *Augustine of Hippo* who represents the culmination of early Latin preaching. *Gregory of Nyssa* (354-430) had a strong desire to win men to Christ.

In the Early Medieval Age, he would want to check the preaching of *St. Patrick* who was the apostle of the Irish and noted as among the great missionary preachers of all time.

In the Central Medieval Age, one could study the preaching of *Bernard of Clairvaux* (1090-1153) who was a Crusade evangelist and possibly the only Crusader who could be considered evangelistic. Many came to Christ as a result of his preaching.

*John Tauler* of Strassburg was one of the most evangelical, devout and effective preachers of his age. His sermons were more like dissertations proceeding in a quiet, orderly way. They would often rise to heights of dramatic energy.

In the Reformation Period, there is of course *Martin Luther,* also a great preacher as well as *John Calvin,* one of the great reformers of the sixteenth century. Finally, in this period, there is *John Knox,* who was the man recognized by historians as having made more of a lasting impact upon his nation's destiny than all others whose lives played a part in its formative years.

In the Early Modern Age, there was *John Bunyan* who became one of the most eminent preachers of his generation. Then there was *Richard Baxter*. Few men have equaled him in persuasiveness and in the urgency of appeal. He is noted as one of the most eminent preachers of the seventeenth century. *Vavasor Powell* has been called the "Whitefield of Wales." Multitudes of converts were won for Christ through his preaching. It was his preaching that was used of God to help prepare the way for the Great Revival in the eighteenth century.

In the Late Modern Age there was *John Wesley* (1703-91). His simple evangelical preaching stirred Britain from one end to the other. *George Whitefield* (1714-70) was one of history's greatest evangelists. Pattison, in his history of preaching, referred to him as the most illustrious of all of the evangelists of the century. *Jonathan Edwards* was a key preacher in the beginning of the Great Awakening. *Christmas Evans* has been referred to as the "Golden-Mouthed Chrysostom of Wales." *Charles G. Finney* certainly deserves a prominent place in the history of evangelistic preaching. *Dwight L. Moody,* whose success rivaled that of Wesley and Whitefield, should be included in the list of evangelists for study. *Charles Haddon Spurgeon* attracted as many people as any preacher in his century. Hundreds were led to Christ through his preaching, and many more were converted to Christ through reading his sermons in print. We might add the names of *Daniel Rowlands* (1713-90) and *Howel Harris* (1714-73) to this list.

In the Contemporary Age, we should list the name of *Reuben A. Torrey* who was used of God to start a revival that swept Europe, the Orient, and the islands of the sea. *William A. Sunday* was the first to conduct evangelistic work on the basis of a large enterprise. *Walter A. Maier* was one of the outstanding radio evangelists of all time. *Billy Graham* has probably preached to more persons than anyone else in the whole history of preaching. *J. Wilbur Chapman* (1859-1918) is remembered as a great soul-winner.

The eighteenth century, the time of the Great Awakening, was probably the greatest century of evangelistic preaching. In the nineteenth century, evangelistic preaching flourished in many countries because of missionary endeavors. It would appear from the survey of the history of preaching that the successful evangelists have been strong biblical preachers.

### GENERAL SUGGESTIONS

Up to this point, we have collected advice from textbooks dealing with evangelistic preaching, from the experienced evangelists of the past, and from general works in evangelism. We now turn to some summarizing, practical suggestions:

1. Evangelistic sermons should be biblical. God has promised to bless His Word. The Holy Spirit speaks through His Word. The message should be permeated with Scripture.
2. Evangelistic sermons should evolve from Scripture rather than being read into Scripture. This is the difference between exegesis and eisegesis. Some of the best passages of Scripture useful in evangelistic preaching are the recorded conversions of Bible characters.
3. Evangelistic sermons should provide spiritual help for the saints as well as for the sinners. It is unfortunate that believers have sometimes found that their spiritual needs are completely overlooked as they have attended evangelistic services.
4. Evangelistic invitations should be clear and specific. Some have felt in the past that certain invitations were not only too long, but also too broad. They may increase the statistics, but may not increase the number of the saved.
5. The evangelistic sermon may profit from an increased number of illustrations over the number in other types of sermons. Illustrations help to make truth clear.
6. The evangelistic sermon can often be based upon a single verse of scripture. The unity of emphasis enhances impression. Such emphasis upon a single verse aids the memory of the listener.
7. The evangelistic sermon should be doctrinal. Too often evangelistic sermons have been thought of as being only a collection of stories. Evangelistic preaching should be based upon the great doctrines of scripture.

8. Evangelistic sermons should be preached on special days of the Christian year, such as Christmas and Easter. Those who make it a point to attend church only on such occasions should be confronted with the call of Christ to repentance and faith.

For the preaching of the cross is to them that perish foolishness; but unto us which are saved it is the power of God. For it is written, I will destroy the wisdom of the wise, and will bring to nothing the understanding of the prudent. Where is the wise? Where is the scribe? Where is the disputer of this world? Hath not God made foolish the wisdom of this world? For after that in the wisdom of God the world by wisdom knew not God, it pleased God by the foolishness of preaching to save them that believe. For the Jews require a sign, and the Greeks seek after wisdom: but we preach Christ crucified, unto the Jews a stumblingblock, and unto the Gentiles foolishness; but unto them which are called, both Jews and Greeks, Christ the power of God, and the wisdom of God. Because the foolishness of God is wiser than men; and the weakness of God is stronger than men.

1 Corinthians 1:18-25

*Reading List*

Austin, William R. *Pastor's Annual 1966*. Grand Rapids: Zondervan, 1966.

Autrey, C. E. *Revivals of the Old Testament*. Grand Rapids: Zondervan, 1960.

Brastow, Lewis O. *The Work of the Preacher*. Boston: Pilgrim, 1914.

Breed, David Riddle. *Preparing to Preach*. New York: Hodder & Stoughton, 1911.

Burrell, David James. *The Sermon: Its Construction and Delivery*. New York: Revell, 1913.

Chirgwin, A. M. *The Bible in World Evangelism*. New York: Friendship, n.d.

Coffin, Henry Sloane. *Communion Through Preaching*. New York: Scribner, 1952.

Dean, Horace F. *Operation Evangelism*. Grand Rapids: Zondervan, 1957.

DeLong, Russell V. *Evangelistic Sermons by Great Evangelists*. Grand Rapids: Zondervan, 1956.

Graves, Henry C. *Lectures on Homiletics.* Philadelphia: Amer. Bapt., 1906.

Johnson, Herrick. *The Ideal Ministry.* New York: Revell, 1913.

Kern, John Adam. *The Ministry to the Congregation.* New York: Jennings & Graham, 1897.

Mott, John R., ed. *Evangelism for the World Today.* New York: Harper, 1938.

Price, J. M., Chapman, J. H., and Carpenter, L. L. *Introduction to Religious Education.* New York: Macmillan, 1932.

Rockey, Carrol J. *Scriptural Evangelism.* Philadelphia: Lutheran Publ., 1925.

Spurgeon, Charles H. *Evangelistic Sermons.* Grand Rapids: Zondervan, 1959.

Stanfield, V. L. *Effective Evangelistic Preaching.* Grand Rapids: Baker, 1965.

Swanson, Lawrence F. *Evangelism in Your Local Church.* Chicago: Harvest, 1959.

Sweazey, George Edgar. *Effective Evangelism.* New York: Harper, 1953.

Whitesell, Faris D. *Evangelistic Preaching and the Old Testament.* Chicago: Moody, 1947.

————. *Sixty-Five Ways to Give an Evangelistic Sermon.* Grand Rapids: Zondervan, 1945.

Wood, Arthur Skevington. *Evangelism, Its Theology and Practice.* Grand Rapids: Zondervan, 1966.

# 8

# Biblical Preaching
# and Its Persuasive Presentation

THE IMPORTANCE of our message and the nature of our calling
make a demand upon us to take advantage of all help available
in making its presentation effective. Research in secular speech
training has provided help in the area of audience analysis and
voice development. It is my conviction that we who are engaged
in the proclamation of the good news should avail ourselves of
this information and thereby improve the effectiveness of our
presentation.

Gene E. Bartlett has reminded us that our primary duty
is not to deliver sermons, but to deliver souls.[1] Yet the tragic
fact is that souls in urgent need of deliverance may never be
delivered because we do not know how to deliver our sermons.
A poor sermon demands a good delivery; a fine sermon deserves
one. And we should be very foolish indeed were we to underestimate or to neglect the vital question of presentation. It is
unfortunate that, with the present decline in emphasis upon
the science of sermon construction, there is also a decline in the
emphasis of speech training for the preacher.

Phillips Brooks preached in London near the beginning of
his ministry. Word was received back in the States following that
experience that he could not be heard past the fourth or fifth
row in the sanctuary. Upon returning to the States, the great
Brooks took speech lessons from then until the close of his
ministry in order that the presentation of the message should
not be handicapped by an inadequate voice.

George W. Truett has been referred to by many as one of

172

the greatest American preachers. To my knowledge, he did not take formal speech training. His articulation and diction were clear, and his voice was resonant. God provided providential circumstances. His preaching to the cowboys on the plains developed his voice. Being forced to move his lips in order to converse with his brother who was handicapped by being deaf and speechless provided the articulation exercises in a very practical setting.

It is unfortunate that many preachers fail to recognize the fact that the presentation of the gospel could be enhanced by gaining some help in the area of speech training. It is also unfortunate that some congregations recognize the need for such training on the part of their preacher, but the preacher refuses to seek such help.

The following colorful statement, taken from the works of Henry Ward Beecher and quoted by Robert T. Oliver, describes the challenge facing the preacher as he stands to present a persuasive message.

> You know how beautifully some men write and how poorly they deliver, how well they prepare their materials and yet their materials, when prepared are of no force whatsoever. They are beautiful arrows, arrows of silver, golden tipped are they and winged with the feathers of the very birds of paradise. But there is no bow to draw the arrows to the head and shoot them strongly home, so they fall out of the sheath down in front of the pulpit or platform.[2]

## THE MEANING OF PERSUASION

What do we mean by *persuasion*? In its generic meaning, it is any verbal method of influencing human conduct. In its specific meaning we refer to influencing human conduct by emotional appeals. It is the instilling, activating, or directing in another individual or other individuals a belief or a type of conduct recommended by the speaker. It was Aristotle who said that there were three sources of persuasive effectiveness. The first, the logical, refers to the facts in the logic of the subject matter. The second, the pathetic, refers to the emotions, biases, and opinions of the audience. The third, the ethical, involves the speaker's personality. These three have been referred to as logos, pathos, and ethos.

## THE TASKS OF THE SPEAKER IN TERMS OF THE AUDIENCE

What is the task of the speaker in terms of the audience? We might list the following five. First, he must catch the atttention of those who are in the audience. Second, he must maintain interest. Third, he must make an impression of the subject and data on the mind and memory of the listener. Fourth, he must motivate. Fifth, he must direct the action. One or more of these tasks will be faced by the speaker as he confronts the various types of audiences.

If he is speaking to a pedestrian audience, one that is moving from place to place, such as a street meeting, he will be interested in catching the attention and maintaining the interest. If he is speaking to a selected audience, one that has been assembled for a common purpose, then his task will be to make an impression of the subject and data on the mind and memory, to motivate to action, and to direct the action. If he is speaking to a concerted audience, one which has an active purpose, then he will be challenged to motivate them to action and direct the action. If he faces an organized audience, such as a scout meeting or a teacher's meeting, then his main task is to direct the action.

## WHY DO SOME SPEECHES FAIL?

Why do some speeches fail? The first reason might be that some speakers fail to distinguish an essay from a speech. It has been said that there is only one similarity between the two, namely they both use words. An essay, is noted for its formality and propriety whereas a speech is more informal. The essay stresses compression and nonrepetition. In a speech, repetition is to be desired since the listeners cannot turn back to a written source and refresh their memory or check on that which they missed. In an essay we can select the right word. But in a speech we cannot stop and select the right word. We must just say it. This means that the speaker must have a good vocabulary at his command. In an essay it is that which you put on paper which really counts. In giving a speech it is that which the audience gets that really matters. When writing an essay it is not necessary to agree with that which you write. When presenting a speech, sincerity is evident. An essay is interested in developing an idea. A speech, however, challenges one to take the idea and develop it in such a way that the audience will be interested in that idea. A speaker is interested in the development of ideas plus the audience reaction. In the essay, the writer must maintain from the start the pattern of the essay. In the speech, however, the speaker can digress, depending upon the reactions of the audience and the emergencies of the moment.

The second reason for the failure of some speeches centers in the fact that they merely elaborate the obvious. There is a lack of originality in the speech.

A third reason for their failure is that sometimes there is an assault on the dignity of the audience. The speaker, for instance, tries to push the audience around. He tells them and does not share with them.

In the fourth place, a typical speech sometimes has no definite thing that it seeks to accomplish, or, in the fifth place, if there is an expected response then the speaker may expect too much from the audience.

At this point it might be wise to consider the objectives which a speaker must keep in mind.

First, he must make the audience aware of him.
Second, he must get the audience to listen to him.
Third, he must get the audience to listen carefully.
Fourth, he must get the audience to have an open mind toward his point of view.
Fifth, he must get the audience to consider what he has to say.
Sixth, he must get the audience to accept his proposal.
Seventh, he must get the audience to take the indicated action.

When a speaker aims at the seventh objective without recognizing the need for meeting the first six objectives as outlined, then he is aiming at too much in a given period of time.

The sixth reason for the failure of speeches is found in the fact that the speakers seem to try to get without giving. Speaking is a challenging and difficult task. It demands all that a man can give to the accomplishment of that task. His enthusiasm, devotedness, and sincerity will go a long way toward accomplishing that which he desires. The audience must sense the fact that he is giving of himself in the delivering of his message.

The seventh reason for the failure of some speeches is found in the fact that the speaker fails to recognize that the audience's power of listening is far more limited than we normally recognize.

The eighth and final reason for the failure of speeches is found in the fact that we try to carry over the push-button technique from the mechanical realm into the realm of human activity. Humans are recalcitrant, they are stubbornly rebellious, and they will not react merely by pushing of a button as you would turn on a light. The speaker is challenged, therefore, to know the techniques of persuasion and the best ways of working with people.

### AUDIENCE ANALYSIS

The public speaker should give attention to audience analysis. An audience is not just an assembly of people. We do not have a true audience unless the receivers of the communication want to hear a message, are capable of receiving it and cooperate in interpreting it. An audience is a group of people gathered for a common purpose and held together for a time, at least, by a common bond. As you are preparing to meet a new audience, try to put yourself in the listener's place. If you were in his position and listening to this message how would you react? Would it hold your attention? Would it move you to action?

The speaker will find it profitable to assess the physical circumstances of the audience. The primary dimensions of audiences and people within the audiences are size, interests, knowledge, belief, and activity levels. The secondary dimensions of an audience are those characteristics of listeners which influence their attendance, interests, knowledge, attitudes, and other behavior and which are subject to modification by communication although they are not its primary objectives. These secondary dimensions include the social and cultural orientation of the audience, the talents and capabilities of the audience, and the adaptation to the audience's expectations of the occasion and the situation. Usually the most significant facts to know about the occasion are the size of the audience and the type of meeting. Webb Garrison says that congregations are made up of individual listeners, each of whom is guided by an elaborate complex of purposes. Some of the more significant motives that lead persons to listen to sermons are loyalty to an institution, habit or no recognized purpose, fellowship, worship, desire for information, respect for traditional authority, curiosity, exhibition, emotional outlet, and personal problems.[3] No matter how important, vital, or interesting we may consider the topic, it must first and foremost contain materials within the comprehension and frame of reference of the particular audience we are addressing. Specifically, we must ask ourselves what kinds of background information does the audience possess, which is directly or indirectly related to this proposition, and what basic attitude does the audience hold toward the subject under consideration? If with no preliminaries at all we told the audience the specific purpose of our speech, what would be their attitude toward it? Usually the most significant things to know about the audience's attitudes toward your topic are whether or not they are already interested, and (if your topic is controversial) are they, in general, for or against your position?

The capacity of the audience to understand is affected by its educational, social, and cultural backgrounds. It is wise, therefore, for the speaker to ask,

1. What general social group does the audience represent?
2. What specific organization does the audience represent?
3. What are the general characteristics of the audience as far as environmental background, general education level, and common interests are concerned?

4. Are the listeners specialists on the subject or at least well informed on it?
5. Or, are they only just superficially informed?
6. Is there a great variation of information or background represented in the audience?
7. Or, finally, are they completely uninformed on the subject to be discussed?

In any speech situation, if you are alert and sensitive, you are likely to meet with surprises that you wouldn't have anticipated no matter how thoroughly you had prepared. Any speech situation is dynamic. Your analysis and evaluation during the situation have to be largely intuitive, without conscious deliberation or directed thinking. The speaker must, therefore, be sensitive to the reactions of his listeners and be ready to adjust accordingly. Gilman, Aly, and Reid have said, "Analyzing an audience is essentially a two-fold problem, namely to discover to what extent the people are alike and to what extent they are different."[4]

The more attention the speaker gives to the study of his audience the more deeply he should realize the infinite variety as well as the essential similarity in the groups he addresses. As he tries to put himself in the place of each listener, he should become more aware of the basic needs and responses of all human beings and seek more understanding of the special problems of individuals and groups.

## Four Types of Audiences

### The apathetic audience

There are basically four types of audiences in terms of their interests and attitudes toward you and your ideas. We give consideration first of all to the apathetic audience. This is the audience which is indifferent toward you and your proposal. The task which confronts you as a speaker is to get their attention and to maintain that attention.

There are certain physical factors which the speaker should be concerned with as he seeks to get the attention of the listeners. First, he will find it advantageous to get them into a polarized situation where they are together. Hopefully this will be at the front of the auditorium so that eye contact can be easily made and maintained. He should avoid using a high stage or platform. The lighting and platform arrangement have an influence. In this regard it is wise to remove as many distractions as possible from the platform, including the chairman of the meeting. If the chairman even moves during the message, the attention of the audience will be directed toward his movements. As far as lighting is concerned, it is wise to have the lights on so that the speaker can see the audience, and so that the audience can see him. It will help in directing the attention of the audience to have a concentration of light centered upon the speaker.

In making the entrance to the platform, it is advised that the speaker avoid hurrying to his place. Once he has arrived at the location from which he is to speak, he should not begin speaking immediately. A slight pause will help to attract the attention of the listeners and will give him an opportunity to become settled. He should remember that the first few minutes of a speech are of great importance.

Any motor activity of the audience with the speaker will help to catch their attention. The normal time or rate of delivery is about 125 words a minute. The speaker should not only vary the rate of speaking, but the force of speaking. He should also make wise use of pause. It has been said that the two causes of ineffectiveness are indirectness and monotone. A rostrum is a bar to effectiveness. The speaker will find it helpful therefore, to leave the rostrum at least on occasion and come in more direct contact with his listeners. A manuscript becomes a barrier between the listeners and the speaker. The speaker should, therefore, become well acquainted with his outline and, hopefully, be able to present his message without notes.

The temperature within the room in which he is speaking will have an influence upon the reception of his message. It is wise to set the thermostat no higher than 65 degrees prior to the arrival of the congregation. As they gather, the temperature within the room will increase to its desired 68 or 70 degrees.

Not only is it important for the speaker to give consideration to a wise adjustment of physical factors if he desires to capture and hold the attention of the audience, but he should also give attention to the choice of ideas to be included in his message. Among the poor ways to begin we might list the presentation of large abstract generalizations, the presentation of a long rambling history of the subject, and the presentation of an apology. Overelaborate preliminaries and definitions will take away the attention of the listeners. It is not wise to begin with the routine beginning in which the speaker gives away the main points of the message. An exception to this last point would be if the speaker is presenting a learned address before a learned society where the knowledge of the points beforehand will be helpful for following the development of the presentation. It is normally not wise to begin with an exposition of the background of knowledge which is necessary for an understanding of the subject.

The speaker will find it helpful to check chapter 16 of the book *Basic Principles of Speech,* written by Sarett and Foster, for a list of approved methods for beginning a message. These authors suggest, among other things, "the relating of the subject to the special interests of the audience, the interpreting of the subject in concrete terms which are familiar to the audience, the creation of curiosity, laying down of a barrage of questions, opening with startling facts, giving an unbelievable statement or paradox, presenting a dramatic treatment of pertinent material, telling a story, presenting an amusing anecdote, opening with a graphic description, using familiar historic instance, referring to a familiar quotation, character or book, and finally using a novel quotation, hypothesis, or prophecy."[5]

The speaker will find it profitable to make use of humorous material. Such material is disarming and provides a relief from the strain of tension. It provides an audience response through laughter. It speeds the making of a point. It provides variety. Humor is a deep human response. Possibly there is no better way to expose minor follies than by laughing at them. The outstanding danger in the use of humor is found in the fact that the audience may come to regard the speaker as being a clown.

The speaker will find that it will be helpful in getting the attention to make use of that which is novel or unusual. The audience will also have a tendency to listen if the speaker presents familiar, homely doings and will listen if he tells the old with a novel twist. The audience will be interested in listening to material which includes action and conflict. They will listen to timely material—that which is relevant and up-to-date. They are interested in "inside stories." An audience normally will listen to material that touches them directly. If the speaker can show how the audience can become participants in a larger enterprise, then they will have a tendency to listen more intently to the speaker. The audience is interested in listening to human interest material—this includes eccentricities of all kinds, such as the town fire house catching on fire. Heart-interest material catches their attention. This would include stories of struggles of unfortunate people, stories of devotion, success after struggle, defeat after struggle, and ironical tragedies.

### THE BELIEVING AUDIENCE

We now turn to the believing audience. This is an audience which has a tendency to accept you and that which you say. The task of the speaker in this situation is to motivate the listeners to action.

The approach to be avoided is that termed "the didactic approach." In this approach the speaker declares what he wants and what he wants done. He has a tendency to be vague, general, and abstract. He uses principles and generalizations. His speech tends to be filled with conclusions without adequate indication of how he arrived at them and the reasons for them. He tends to assume that the audience can make the leap from the principles to the application. The approach lacks the art of attractiveness and follows the typical textbook format structure.

The type of approach which should be used is termed "the dramatic approach." In this approach the speaker tries to get the point of the message in terms of the living experience of his people. He tends to present what he has to say with a minimum of principles and a maximum of illustrations.

He should employ visual aids. Theoretically, every idea can

be visualized. However, dangers oftimes prevalent with such visual aids must be avoided. One of these is to make the visual aid so interesting that the listeners forget the message and remember only the visual aid. There is also the danger of having the visual aid for its own sake. The speaker must make certain that the visual aid is visible to all the people in the audience.

The dramatic approach encourages audience participation. As the speaker seeks to do this he should be sure to avoid embarrassing any of the listeners. The approach encourages the massing of facts and details. It encourages the use of examples and anecdotes. Rather than presenting one's point flatly and bluntly, this approach encourages the use of indirection. The speaker will want to make use of comparisons, similes, and metaphors. A comparison is an attempt to compare objects which have many qualities in common. A simile, the most used figure of speech, is an attempt to compare things essentially unlike except in certain respects. A simile is an economical figure of speech. It allows you to say two things in place of one. It gives a good opportunity to bring freshness to the speech. A metaphor is the figure of speech which Aristotle thought was the most important. It is an imaginative identification of one object with another. It is the declaration, not that one object is like another, but that one object is another. The metaphor is a concealed simile.

It is obvious that the metaphor has more "punch" than the simile. The simile has always a *like* or an *as* in it, and the *like* and the *as* tend to weaken it. We can see that at once if we put it to a practical test. Suppose Jesus would have said, "I am like a door." How greatly that would have diminished the force of the figure! He did not. He said, "I am the door." The simile would have been slightly ludicrous; the metaphor is suggestively luminous.

The eighth and final characteristic of the dramatic approach stresses the placing of emphasis upon the telling details. These are little details that the average person has a tendency to overlook. The speaker should be specific in his description of each major item referred to in the speech. Generalizations tend to decrease the interest. Specifics tend to increase interest.

## THE HOSTILE AUDIENCE

The third type of audience is the hostile audience. This audience may be hostile to you, or to your ideas. It is wise for a speaker to give consideration to methods which he may use to establish his authority to speak before such an audience. He may do this first by invoking the authority of others. He may be a spokesman for another person, just a mouthpiece; and he stands and tells the listeners that he just wants to tell them what great men of today think and say. In such a presentation, he will adopt a flat delivery. If he is quoting an authority, he will want to be able to prove that his authority is qualified to speak on the issue. In doing this, he may want to reveal that his authority has one or more of the official signs of respectability: (1) he has written a textbook in that general area; (2) he belongs to recognized organizations in that area of consideration; (3) his educational background is adequate within that area; or (4) he is a professor or teacher of that subject. He will want to show that his authority is in agreement with authorities of equal stature. He may want to establish the special competence of the authority which he is quoting. He will do this by showing that his authority is in a position to know the facts. He will want to establish the credibility of his authority by showing how many times he has been correct in the past.

The speaker may invoke his own personal authority. He can establish his prestige through his force and vitality as a speaker, his poise and confidence, kindness, sympathy, compassion, sincerity, and earnestness. His enthusiasm will be an important factor. The thoroughness of his preparation will be a good, positive factor.

## THE DOUBTFUL AUDIENCE

The audience classified as a doubtful audience has accumulated facts but have not as yet formed definite opinions. When a speaker prepares to make a presentation before such an audience, he should know how to develop theories, make predictions, and talk factually.

A theory is an attempt to provide a statement that will cover the aspects of phenomena which seem to be observable. Any theory is a matter of probability and combines a number of inferences. When a speaker draws a conclusion before a doubtful audience, he must assure the audience concerning the validity of his basic theory.

As a speaker makes predictions based on human speculation, he should recognize that any such prediction is merely a probability. He must assure his audience of the degree of control which he has over the variables involved in the prediction.

The effective speaker before a doubtful audience must be able to speak factually. A study of the contributions made by general semantics will be of assistance at this point. This discipline combines a study of the facts of the world, the words which express the facts, and the human evaluation which results from the combination of facts and words. One of the earliest books in this study was written by Alfred Korzybski entitled *Science and Sanity*. The book entitled *Language Habits and Human Affairs* by Irving J. Lee is extremely profitable for study. Logical positivism is the philosophical foundation for general semantics. The sermonizer should remember this as he studies the material. He can profit from many of their findings though he does not agree with their basic philosophical approach. The general semanticist offers the following suggestions which may prove helpful to the preacher:

1. Avoid stating inferences as though they were facts.
2. Since there is complexity in all things and since all speaking actually involves abstracting details from that complexity, avoid giving the impression to the listeners that what you say on a subject is all that could possibly be said.
3. Avoid making reference to items which change without dating your statements.
4. Avoid oversimplification in talking by using terms which describe only extremes and limits.
5. Recognize that there is a type of speaking which is not aimed at conveying information but is rather only an attempt to

reach out through speech and make contact with another person. Such speech is called phatic communion.

These and many other suggestions will assist the sermonizer in making his message more persuasive to the doubtful audience.

## BASIC PRINCIPLES OF SERMON PRESENTATION

A preacher should give careful attention not only to the analysis of the audience to which the message is directed but also to speech factors involved in sermon presentation.

When Hugh Latimer was preaching once before Henry VIII, he was overheard to say to himself as he mounted the pulpit stairs: "Latimer! Latimer! Latimer! You must take care what you say, for the great King Henry VIII is here!" Then for a moment he paused and was heard to add, "Latimer! Latimer! Latimer! You must take care what you say, for the King of kings is here!"

The seven basic principles of speech as set forth by Sarett and Foster have relevance for pulpit speech as well as for general public speaking. These principles stress that speech should not be for exhibition but rather for communication. The ultimate end of the techniques of speech should be the winning of a response. The effective speaker will use the techniques of speech in order to bring attention to a high peak on the response for which he is striving. Effective speech is disarming in its apparent spontaneity, ease, and simplicity. The speaker must be an able person in a good emotional state, with a good attitude toward himself and toward his audience. He should be aware of the fact that impressions of the speaker are often derived from sources of which the audience is often unaware. The final, basic principle states that effective speech results in part from free, properly motivated, bodily action.[6]

## ANIMATION IN SERMON DELIVERY

Effective speech is characterized by an alertness and animation that grows out of the speaker's attitude toward his total speaking situation. The alertness and animation will be revealed in his general tonus of body, alertness of bearing, flexibility of voice, expressiveness of face and eyes, and the variety in the total delivery pattern. There are several factors which seem to increase one's animation of delivery: (1) an intense belief in one's subject, (2) a confidence in one's ability to present one's subject, (3) an eagerness to address that particular audience, (4) a knowledge of the opening sentences of the message, (5) a fervent desire to aid one's listeners, and (6) the possession of an abundance of material on the subject of the message.

### GESTURES: VISIBLE SYMBOLS OF SPEECH

Gesturing is an important factor in the effective presentation of a message. Effective gesturing is characterized by a quality of purpose which might be called intention. This means that the good speaker intends his actions to reveal his true feelings. Irrelevant gestures often serve to confuse or belie the meaning of our words. The speaker should rid his mind of the idea that it is wrong to gesture. He should practice for that freedom of action which is normal for him. Effective bodily action reflects motivation and demonstrates a clear measure of control.

Great speakers of the past have given considerable attention to delivery. They have gone to the seashore, to a plowed field, to an attic, or even to a stable in order to find an isolated location presentations will not only serve to develop one's speaking style where they might rehearse without being disturbed. Among the more recent and effective practices is rehearsing before a mirror. A message should be delivered orally at least twice before being presented in final form before a congregation. These practice and expand one's vocabulary, but they also will give opportunity to adjust the gesturing to the wording. The recording and playing back of the message on a tape recorder is profitable.

Gestures are referred to in speech books as visible symbols of speech. Conventional gestures are those which are used to incite strong reactions and to reinforce important ideas. Autistic gestures on the other hand are meaningless gestures which serve to indicate the inner feelings of the speaker rather than to reinforce important ideas. They are normally mere nervous reactions on the part of the speaker.

Action employed in connection with speaking should be spontaneous. Gestures should grow out of the speech rather than being tacked onto the speech. The speaker should avoid an over-use of any one gesture. Variety of action should be one of his goals. The effective speaker must avoid random activity, immobility, overrelaxation, and a fixed facial expression.

When a speaker discovers that he has a habit of delivery which demands a change, he should remember that there are three steps in changing a habit. The first step is to have a motivation for a change. The second is to be aware of the difference between the right and wrong habit. The third step is the suppression of that which is undesirable. The good speaker should be on the alert for those habits in gesturing which should be changed since they are hindrances rather than helps in the presentation of the message.

In past days when elocution flourished as a method of speech training, specific systems of gestures were devised, and a tremendous amount of supervised practice was employed in order to execute the gestures in a precise manner. It implied that there was just one proper way to make a gesture. In more recent days the speakers have been encouraged to employ in public address the gestures which they would normally employ in conversation. Gestures can be used to assist in description and also to provide emphasis.

### Phonetics: Audible Syombols of Speech

In presenting a message, the speaker should not only be concerned about the visible symbols of speech, namely the gestures, but also about the audible symbols of speech. Until 1888, speech was studied on an unscientific basis. This made it extremely difficult to correct speech difficulties and to study language in general. In 1888 the International Phonetic Alphabet was developed. This alphabet provides a sign for each sound. In our English alphabet, we have twenty-six letters and some forty different sounds. The diacritical markings which appear in our dictionaries as supposed aids to pronunciation lack consistency. Phonetics is the science of speech sounds and provides a basis for the technical study of language. It unravels the confusion of letters and sounds as well as providing a consistent guide for pronunciation.

Articulation is the process of having two parts of the vocal mechanism come together in order that a consonant can be formed. Public speakers often have difficulty in pronouncing *d*'s and *t*'s that come at the end of a word. Why? One reason may be due to the fact that the speaker is too careless in speaking and just doesn't take the trouble to lift the tip of his tongue to the alveolar ridge at the front of the mouth located just behind the upper front teeth. Whenever we make a *t* or *d* sound the tongue tip goes to that ridge, holds the air there for just a moment and then lets it explode. When this explosion of air takes place we have a *t* sound, and when vocal cord vibration is combined with that explosion of air, we have a *d* sound. This is the type of assistance which is provided for speech correction through a knowledge of phonetics.

The sibilant or hissing sounds in English provide pronunciation obstacles for many speakers. The most common of these sounds is that of the *s* sound. The scientific study of the sounds of English notes that the *s* sound when formed correctly involves the tip of the tongue being directed toward the same alveolar ridge located behind the front teeth. The tip of the tongue is separated from that ridge just far enough so that the flow of air can pass over the tip of the tongue, past the teeth ridge, and down behind the front teeth until it is emitted. If a tooth is missing, the flow of air will follow the opening left by the extracted tooth and will produce a hissing sound. If there are jagged edges on the front teeth these will tend to produce a whistle on the *s* sound. Simple problems of articulation can often be corrected through utilization of information gained in a study of phonetics. More than 70 percent of the speech difficulties are articulatory in nature.

### RELAXATION AND SERMON PRESENTATION

Voice quality is that which distinguishes one voice from another. It is a matter of the production of tone itself. The chief resonators of sound are the mouth, the pharynx or back wall of the mouth, and the nasal passages. By making that back wall of the mouth larger or smaller, harder or softer by changing the tonicity of the muscles, we can change the voice quality. We see therefore that voice quality centers largely in the realm of relaxation. Nasality is one of the common voice quality faults. It appears in speech when sounds other than the *m, n,* and *ng* sounds are emitted through the nasal cavity. Tension within the vocal mechanism will often evidence itself in nasal speech. If the pitch of the voice is too high, this may be due to tension. This is one of many speech disorders which can at least partially be corrected through relaxation.

Since relaxation is so important to good speech, the public speaker would be wise to obtain one or two good books on the subject. Some of these are available on the popular book counters, and others may be obtained from the public library. The first step in relaxation is the recognition of tension. Once the tension is located, then one can work on alleviating it. General relaxation of the vocal area may be obtained by having the head rotate on the axis of the neck as though it were a heavy weight on the end of a rope tethered to the backbone. The head can be rotated to the left and to the right in a slow, rhythmical fashion. Tension may be removed from the arms by swinging them rhythmically forward and backward from the shoulders. One should be sure that the joints of the fingers, wrists, and elbows are relaxed. The hands can be closed tightly and then forced open to a spread position. By continuing this process and then later by swinging the hands loosely at the wrist, one can remove much of the tension from the hands. Since the body works as a unit in the speaking process, it is important to make certain that not just the vocal mechanism is relaxed but also the other portions of the body are relaxed.

It is important that the speaker have an understanding of the breathing cycle. As the speaker inhales, the diaphragm expands; and as he exhales, it contracts. Unless this cycle is maintained, the speaker will have inadequate breath support for vocalization. It is especially important that the speaker learn to control the flow of outgoing air. Good breathing for speech involves controlled exhalation. The problem is not to get more air into the lungs but to control the use of the air which is already available. If the speaker desires to develop breath control, breathing exercises should be used in connection with the process of speaking.

ORAL INTERPRETATION OF SCRIPTURE

Speech training is profitable in developing an effective sermon presentation and also profitable in presenting the scripture reading of the worship service. Too little attention has been paid in the past to the oral interpretation of the Scripture.

There are several qualifications which one should have in order to be a good interpreter of the printed page. These include keen observation powers, spontaneity, a keen imagination, a good command of poise, an ability to let oneself go in the midst of the material, an intense realization of the meaning of the author's words, and finally an awareness of sound, words, and rhythm.

In order to be a good reader of the printed page, one must be able to discern the complete meaning of the passage being read. This involves recognizing the author's purpose and if possible a bit of knowledge of the author himself. The reader should seek to discover the dominant unity of the passage. He must try finally to develop a total bodily response to the passage. He should avoid major gestures as he reads.

There are several problem areas in this process of interpreting the printed page of Scripture to the congregation. The first problem area involves the correlation of punctuation and oral reading. The purpose of punctuation points is to assist the reader in understanding the writer's meaning. The punctuation points help the reader get the meaning but are not there to control his presentation of the passage to the listener. It should therefore be remembered that in oral reading the comma does not necessarily indicate a pause.

The second problem area involves word meaning. The good reader will pay attention to the denotation of the word which is the exact dictionary meaning, but he will go beyond this to the connotation of the word which refers to the dictionary meaning as it is modified by the context in which the word appears.

The next problem area in interpretation involves the process of grouping. This is the act of breaking up the text into ideas. The word is a grammatical unit, but the idea is the speech unit. In the act of grouping, verbs are never grouped alone since the mind always supplies someone or something with the verb. Adjectives are grouped alone if they stand in contrast. No absolute rule can be laid down for the length of a speech unit. Common sense is the only guide. Normally the longer the speech unit the better. Grouping is important since it gives the speaker time to catch his breath while reading, it gives the speaker time to formulate his next thought group, it gives time for the meaning to sink into the mind of the listener, and it helps to maintain the rhythmic flow of the sentence.

When determining the length of the thought group it is wise to consider the complexity of the material. The more complex the material, the shorter the thought group. The reader should consider the size and character of the audience. Shorter thought groups are normally more effective when speaking or reading before a large audience. The third factor to be considered is the purpose of the reader. If he wants the listener to get the minute details of the material, then he should use shorter thought grouping.

Before the reader can convey the meaning of a passage to the listener, he must first grasp the meaning himself. How can one discover the meaning of a passage in order that he be able to read it more effectively? The following suggestions may prove helpful: (1) read the selection in its entirety in order to discover its one complete idea; (2) pay special attention to the topic sentence; (3) watch for repeated words and phrases; (4) watch for thought summaries within the passage; (5) watch for contrasts and comparisons; (6) take note of the figures of speech, and check their meaning to determine why they were used; (7) formulate a paraphrased edition of the passage.

The effective oral reader must understand the relationship between meter and rhythm. Meter is any specific form of poetic rhythm. Rhythm basically means flow. Rhythm is a natural characteristic of all spoken language. A factor which is especially important in maintaining good rhythm in both reading and speaking involves the recognition of what the speech scientist calls strong and weak forms. A strong form is an accented syllable. The oral reader can survey the- passage to be read, mark, and identify each syllable which appears in an accented postion. He then glides over the syllables which are in an unaccented position as lightly as possible. The unaccented syllables are considered weak forms.

An effective use of intonation patterns will improve one's oral reading. Intonation is the rise and fall of the pitch of the voice. The reader should be especially concerned with the last section of each sentence. A falling inflection at the end of a sentence indicates a completed thought, a command given, a decision reached, or a question asked which employs an interrogative word. A rising inflection implies an unfinished thought, a simple surprise, doubt or uncertainty, or finally a question asked without an interrogative word. The level intonation implies a suspended thought, amazement, wonder, or deep controlled emotion. A circumflex inflection characterizing a larger group of words denotes sarcasm, scorn, or the complication of surprise and doubt.

The final problem to which we want to give consideration is that of discovering ways to emphasize that which needs emphasis within the passage. The most popular method is that of the inflection of the voice. Another means of emphasis is by the use of the pause. The anticipatory pause occurs before that to which the reader desires to call attention and the deliberate pause after the item emphasized. Emphasis can be provided by changing the tempo or the volume. The altering of the intonation pattern helps to provide emphasis. The use of force, hitting a word with the voice, provides emphasis. Two additional methods of providing emphasis are by the prolongation of vowels and the intensification of rhythm.

## General Speech Delivery

The concept of conversational quality has been advocated by many. In secular speaking, the conversational approach to public speaking was advocated by James Winans of Cornell University. In the area of pulpit address, it was promoted by Phillips Brooks. This approach to public address can be likened to a gentleman conversing with his friend. He merely turns up the volume as he stands before the audience.

The delivery of a sermon is a spiritual work for which there is need for the constant help of the Spirit of God. This will tend to provide earnestness and the note of authority. Poor delivery may be the result of poor preparation, the pressure of time, the unwise use of humor, or the lack of spiritual fire. Spiritual preparation is a vital factor in persuasive sermon delivery. Emotional preaching, in the good sense of the word, should be advocated. There are both the logical and the emotional appeals. Logic is primarily concerned with information while emotion is closely linked with action. There is no necessary conflict between intellectual honesty and emotional fervor. Enthusiasm for the message is a prerequisite to vital preaching.

The preacher's chief tool of his trade is his voice, yet the development of the instrument itself and of skill in its use is shamefully neglected in seminary education. Three conditions are necessary to have and maintain a good voice: proper physical equipment, good mental attitude, and adequate spiritual adjustment.

Phelps said "The crowning gift of the speaker in public is summed up in a phrase of three words: *Earnestness of purpose*."[7] Such an emphasis takes us back to the point of beginning as set forth in 2 Corinthians 5:1-21. We have a message. We have adequate motivation. We have scriptural measurements for our ministry. We are messengers for God. We are ambassadors therefore on behalf of Christ; and our ambassadorial message borne to men from God must be "Get reconciled to God" (2 Co 5:20).

Biblical preaching in today's world demands that the ambassador for Jesus Christ be willing to pay whatever price the task demands. The King's message must go through.

A parable of this truth is found in the experience of Walter Vivian, an official of the Columbia Broadcasting Company. It was on a January morning in 1930. King George's speech to the London Naval Conference was to be broadcast. Vivian discovered a wire connection had been severed. The repair would take thirty minutes, but the time was not available. To meet the crisis, he gripped the broken wire, one end in each hand, and thereby restored the current. In doing so, his body was shocked and his hand severely burned by the 250 volt charge.[8] Whatever be the price, the King's message must go through.

Toil on, faint not, keep watch, and pray,
Be wise the erring soul to win;
Go forth into the world's highway,
Compel the wanderer to come in.
Toil on, and in thy toil rejoice,
For toil comes rest, for exile's home;
Soon shalt thou hear the Bridegroom's voice,
The midnight peal, Behold I come.

HORATIUS BONAR

## Reading List

Bettinghaus, Erwin P. *Persuasive Communication.* New York: Holt, Rinehart & Winston, 1968.

Brembeck, W. L. and Howell, W. S. *Persuasion, a Means of Social Control.* Englewood Cliffs, N.J.: Prentice, 1952.

DeWire, Harry A. *The Christian as Communicator.* Philadelphia: Westminster, 1961.

Garrison, Webb B. *Creative Imagination in Preaching.* Nashville: Abingdon, 1960.

——————. *Preacher and His Audience.* Westwood, N.J.: Revell, 1954.

Hayakawa, S. I. *Language in Thought and Action.* New York: Harcourt Brace, 1949.

Hollingsworth, H. L. *Psychology of the Audience.* New York: American, 1935.

Johnson, Wendel. *People in Quandries.* New York: Harper, 1940.

Korzybski, Alfred. *Science and Sanity.* Lakeville, Connecticut: The International Non-Aristotelian Library, 1948.

Lee, Irving J. *Language Habits in Human Affairs.* New York: Harper, 1941.

Lesch, Gomer R. *Creative Christian Communication.* Nashville: Broadman, 1965.

Lewis, Ralph L. *Speech for Persuasive Preaching.* Berne, Indiana: Economy, 1968.

Marsh, Patrick O. *Persuasive Speaking.* New York: Harper & Row, 1967.

McLaughlin, Raymond W. *Communication for the Church.* Grand Rapids: Zondervan, 1968.

Monroe, Alan H. *Principles and Types of Speech.* Chicago: Scott, Foresman, 1962.

Oliver, Robert T. *Persuasive Speaking.* New York: Longmans, Green, 1950.

————. *Psychology of Persuasive Speech.* New York: Longmans, Green, 1948.

Phillips, Arthur Edward. *Effective Speaking.* Chicago: Newton, 1917.

Sarett, Lew, and Foster, W. T. *Basic Principles of Speech.* Boston: Houghton Mifflin, 1946.

Sleeth, Ronald E. *Persuasive Preaching.* New York: Harper & Row, 1956.

Stevenson, Dwight and Diehl, Charles F. *Reaching People from the Pulpit.* New York: Harper & Row, 1958.

Winans, James. *Public Speaking.* New York: Century, 1926.

————. *Speech-Making.* New York: Appleton-Century, 1938.

# Notes

CHAPTER 1

1. Henry Sloane Coffin, *Communion Through Preaching*, p. 2.
2. Pierre Berton, *The Comfortable Pew*, pp. 96-97.
3. Donald G. Miller, *The Way to Biblical Preaching*, p. 7.
4. Helmut Thielicke, *The Trouble with the Church*, p. 2.
5. Kyle Haselden, *The Urgency of Preaching*, p. 18.
6. Jack D. Sanford, *Make Your Preaching Relevant*, p. 17.
7. Ibid., p. 18.
8. Wallace E. Fisher, *Preaching and Parish Renewal*, p. 26.
9. James S. Stewart, *Heralds of God*, p. 55.
10. George W. Truett, *The Inspiration of Ideals*, pp. 157-58.
11. Faris D. Whitesell, *The Art of Biblical Preaching*, p. 16.
12. Sanford, p. 20.
13. Merrill R. Abbey, *Living Doctrines in a Vital Pulpit*, p. 124.
14. G. Campbell Morgan, *Preaching*, p. 22.
15. John Dover, "The Training of the First Preachers," *Preacher's Quarterly* 14, no. 3 (September 1968): 163.
16. John H. Jowett, *The Preacher: His Life and Work*, p. 19.
17. Ian MacPherson, *The Burden of the Lord*, p. 60.
18. Ibid., p. 20.
19. T. Harwood Pattison, *The Making of the Sermon*, p. 3.
20. MacPherson, p. 75.
21. Austin Phelps, *The Theory of Preaching*, p. 1.
22. Ibid., pp. 1-14.
23. James M. Hoppin, *Homiletics*, p. 444.
24. Paul S. Rees, "Five Key Elements of Effective Sermons," in *How To Prepare and Deliver Better Sermons*, pp. 21-27.
25. Ian MacPherson, *The Art of Illustrating Sermons*, p. 186.
26. M. Reu, *Homiletics*, p. 129.
27. Sanford, pp. 79-80.
28. Corwin Roach, *Preaching Values in the Bible*, p. 115.

CHAPTER 2

1. Lloyd M. Perry, "Trends and Emphases in the Philosophy, Materials, and Methodology of American Protestant Homiletical Education as Established by a Study of Selected Trade and Textbooks Published between 1834 and 1954" (Ph.D. diss., Northwestern U., 1961), p. 483.
2. Ralph G. Turnbull, ed., *Baker's Dictionary of Practical Theology*, pp. 74-81.

3. Andrew W. Blackwood, *The Preparation of Sermons*, p. 20.
4. Charles W. Koller, *Sermons Preached Without Notes*, p. 7.
5. Langdon Gilkey, *How the Church Can Minister to the World Without Losing Itself*, p. 3.
6. Koller, pp. 61-63.
7. Ernest Fremont Tittle, *The Foolishness of Preaching*, pp. 304-5.
8. Lloyd M. Perry and Robert D. Culver, *How to Search the Scriptures*, pp. 36-38.
9. Ibid., pp. 256-260.
10. Ian MacPherson, *The Art of Illustrating Sermons*, p. 102.
11. Quoted in George W. Truett, *The Inspiration of Ideals*, pp. 33-34.

CHAPTER 3

1. John Kelman, *The War and Preaching*, p. 151.
2. F. R. Webber, *A History of Preaching in Britain and America*, 1:345-46.
3. Lloyd M. Perry, *Biblical Sermon Guide*, pp. 29-30.
4. Ian Maclaren, *The Cure of Souls*, p. 41.
5. Alfred E. Garvie, *The Christian Preacher*, pp. 433-39.
6. Charles W. Koller, *Expository Preaching Without Notes*, pp. 108-12.
7. Ian MacPherson, *The Art of Illustrating Sermons*, p. 187.

CHAPTER 4

1. Charles H. Spurgeon, *Great Pulpit Masters*, 2:10-11.
2. Austin Phelps, *The Theory of Preaching*, p. 33.
3. Quoted in Ian MacPherson, *The Burden of the Lord*, p. 87.
4. Lloyd M. Perry, *Biblical Sermon Guide*, pp. 63-67.
5. Ibid.
6. Clyde Reid, *The Empty Pulpit*, p. 83.
7. Harvey Cox, *The Secular City*, p. 122.
8. Reid, p. 90.
9. Reuel L. Howe, *The Miracle of Dialogue*, p. 37.
10. William D. Thompson, *A Listener's Guide to Preaching*, p. 32.
11. J. Leslie Tizard, *Preaching: The Art of Communication*, p. 30.
12. Harry Emerson Fosdick. "What Is the Matter with Preaching?" *Harper's Magazine*, no. 157 (July, 1928), p. 137.
13. Wesley Pinkham, "The Role of the Pastor as a Change Agent in the Middle Class, Conservative Church in Suburbia" (Th.M. thesis, Trinity Evang. Div. School, 1970), pp. 64-87.
14. William D. Thompson and Gordon C. Bennett, *Dialogue Preaching*, p. 9.
15. Ibid., p. 31.
16. Ibid., pp. 24-64.

CHAPTER 5

1. W. M. MacGregor, *The Making of a Preacher*, p. 50.
2. F. B. Meyer, *Expository Preaching: Plans and Methods*, p. 35.
3. Robert McCracken, *The Making of a Sermon*, p. 51.

4. J. Leslie Tizard, *Preaching: The Art of Communication*, p. 22.
5. Jesse J. McNeil, *The Preacher-Prophet in Mass Society*, p. 70.
6. Walter R. Bowie, *Preaching*, p. 138.
7. Charles Smith, *Biblical Authority for Modern Preaching*, p. 96.
8. F. R. Webber, *A History of Preaching in Britain and America*, 2:30.
9. Ibid., 3:136.
10. Ibid., 2:653-54.
11. Ronald E. Sleeth, *Proclaiming the Word*, p. 86.
12. Lloyd M. Perry, "Trends and Emphases in the Philosophy, Materials, and Methodology of American Protestant Homiletical Education as Established by a Study of Selected Trade and Textbooks Published Between 1834 and 1954" (Ph.D. diss., Northwestern U., 1961), p. 412.
13. Clarence S. Roddy, "The Classification of Sermons," in *Baker's Dictionary of Practical Theology*, ed. R. G. Turnbull, p. 61.
14. As quoted in McCracken, p. 37.
15. J. H. McBurney and K. G. Hance, *Discussion in Human Affairs*, pp. 65-68.
16. Arthur L. Teikmanis, *Preaching and Pastoral Care*, p. 17.

CHAPTER 6

1. Phillips Brooks, *Yale Lectures on Preaching*, p. 129.
2. Andrew W. Blackwood, *Doctrinal Preaching for Today*, p. 51
3. M. Reu, *Homiletics*, p. 151.
4. Lloyd M. Perry, "Trends and Emphases in the Philosophy, Materials, and Methodology of American Protestant Homiletical Education as Established by a Study of Selected Trade and Textbooks Published between 1834 and 1954." (Ph.D. diss., Northwestern U., 1961), p. 483.
5. Lewis O. Brastow, *The Work of the Preacher*, p. 176.
6. Alan Richardson, *Christian Apologetics*, p. 19.
7. Gerald Ray Jordan, *You Can Preach*, pp. 221-23.
8. Blackwood, p. 151.
9. William W. Ayer, "The Art of Effective Preaching," *Bibliotheca Sacra* 124 (Jan.-Mar. 1967): 30-41.
10. Gerald J. Jud, *Crisis in the Church*, pp. 46-47.
11. Merril R. Abbey, *Living Doctrines in a Vital Pulpit*, p. 42.
12. Faris D. Whitesell, *Power in Expository Preaching*, p. 92.
13. James Braga, *How to Prepare Bible Messages*, p. 174.
14. John Edward Baird, *Preparing for Platform and Pulpit*, p. 120.
15. John W. Etter, *The Preacher and His Sermon*, p. 372.
16. David J. Randolph, *The Renewal of Preaching*, p. 89.
17. Ibid., p. 75.
18. Charles W. Koller, *Expository Preaching Without Notes*, p. 51.
19. Ilion T. Jones, *Principles and Practice of Preaching*, pp. 150-51.
20. Whitesell, pp. 93-94.
21. George W. Hervey, *Christian Rhetoric*, p. 299.
22. Ebenezer Porter, *Lectures on Homiletics and Preaching, and on Public Prayer*, p. 159.
23. T. Harwood Pattison, *The Making of the Sermon*, pp. 179.
24. S. T. Sturtevant, *The Preacher's Manual*, p. 137.
25. Jeff Brown, *A Handbook for the Preacher at Work*, p. 40.

26. Henry S. Coffin, *Communion Through Preaching*, p. 62.
27. Jean Jacques von Allmen, *Preaching and Congregation*, pp. 52-53.
28. Herbert H. Farmer, *The Servant of the Word*, p. 81.
29. David R. Breed, *Preparing to Preach*, p. 248.
30. Ralph L. Lewis, *Speech for Persuasive Preaching*, p. 90.
31. Breed, pp. 275-76.
32. Faris D. Whitesell, *Power in Expository Preaching*, p. 93.
33. Reu, p. 362.
34. Ilion T. Jones, *Principles and Practice of Preaching*, p. 133.
35. As quoted by Ian MacPherson, *The Art of Illustrating Sermons*, p. 129.
36. Ibid, p. 181.

*CHAPTER 7*

1. As quoted by J. M. Price, J. H. Chapman, and L. L. Carpenter, *Introduction to Religious Education*, p. 180.
2. John R. Mott, ed., *Evangelism for the World Today*, p. 96.
3. Henry C. Graves, *Lectures on Homiletics*, p. 125.
4. As quoted by Graves, p. 125.
5. John Adam Kern, *The Ministry to the Congregation*, p. 453.
6. Lewis Brastow, *The Work of the Preacher*, p. 232.
7. David J. Burrell, *The Sermon: Its Construction and Delivery*, p. 102.
8. As quoted by Carrol J. Rockey, *Scriptural Evangelism*, p. 18.
9. Horace F. Dean, *Operation Evangelism*, p. 51.
10. Ibid., p. 60.
11. David R. Breed, *Preparing to Preach*, p. 409.
12. Andrew W. Blackwood, *Evangelism in the Home Church*, pp. 72-88.
13. Ozora S. Davis, *Evangelistic Preaching*, pp. 62-68.
14. Rockey, p. 18.
15. Herrick Johnson, *The Ideal Ministry*, pp. 471-75.
16. V. L. Stanfield, *Effective Envangelistic Preaching*, pp. 22-24.
17. Brastow, p. 245.
18. Robert Menzies, *Preaching and Pastoral Evangelism*, pp. 32-51.
19. Stanfield, pp. 24-25.
20. A. S. Hoyt, *The Preacher: His Person, Message, and Method*, pp. 273-75.
21. Brastow, p. 247.
22. R. W. Dale, *Nine Lectures on Preaching*, pp. 204-8.
23. Stanfield, pp. 32-35.
24. Faris D. Whitesell, *Sixty-Five Ways to Give an Evangelistic Invitation*, pp. 11-21.
25. C. E. Autrey, *Revivals of the Old Testament*, pp. 125-31.
26. Stanfield, p. 28.
27. George Edgar Sweazey, *Effective Evangelism*, p. 174.
28. Whitesell, pp. 22-30.
29. Autrey, pp. 131-34.
30. Ibid., pp. 131-34.
31. Edgar Whitaker Work, *Every Minister His Own Evangelist*, pp. 39-41.
32. See Lloyd M. Perry, *Biblical Sermon Guide*, pp. 63-67.
33. Ibid., pp. 67-69.
34. Ibid., pp. 79-80.

CHAPTER 8

1. Quoted in Ian MacPherson, *The Art·of Illustrating Sermons,* p. 184.
2. Robert T. Oliver, *The Psychology of Persuasive Speech,* p. 305.
3. Webb B. Garrison, *The Preacher and His Audience,* pp. 26-43.
4. Wilbur E. Gilman, Bower Aly, and Loren Reid, *The Fundamentals of Speaking,* p. 379.
5. Lew Sarett and W. T. Foster, *Basic Principles of Speech,* pp. 384-420.
6. Ibid., pp. 13-51.
7. Arthur S. Phelps, *Speaking in Public,* p. 152.
8. James W. Clarke, *Dynamic Preaching,* pp. 102-3.

# Bibliography

Abbey, Merrill R. *Living Doctrines in a Vital Pulpit.* Nashville: Abingdon, 1965.

Alexander, James Waddel. *Thoughts on Preaching, Being Contributions to Homiletics.* New York: Scribner, 1861.

Allen, Arthur. *The Art of Preaching.* New York: Philosophical Library, 1943.

Augustine, Aurelius. *On Christian Doctrine.* Trans. and intro. by D. W. Robertson, Jr. New York: Liberal Arts, 1958.

Autrey, C. E. *Basic Evangelism.* Grand Rapids: Zondervan, 1959.

——————. *Revivals of the Old Testament.* Grand Rapids: Zondervan, 1960.

Ayer, William W. "The Art of Effective Preaching." *Bibliotheca Sacra* 124:30-41.

Baird, John Edward. *Preparing for Platform and Pulpit.* Nashville: Abingdon, 1968.

Berton, Pierre. *The Comfortable Pew.* Philadelphia: Lippincott, 1965.

Blackwood, Andrew W. *Doctrinal Preaching for Today.* New York: Abingdon-Cokesbury, 1956.

——————. *Evangelism in the Home Church.* New York: Abingdon-Cokesbury, 1942.

——————. *The Preparation of Sermons.* Nashville: Abingdon-Cokesbury, 1946.

Bowie, Walter R. *Preaching.* New York: Abingdon, 1954.

Braga, James. *How to Prepare Bible Messages.* Portland, Oreg.: Multnomah, 1969.

Brastow, Lewis Orsmond. *The Work of the Preacher.* Boston: Pilgrim, 1914.

Breed, David Riddle. *Preparing to Preach.* New York: Hodder & Stoughton, 1911.

Broadus, John A. *A Treatise on the Preparation and Delivery of Sermons.* New York: Harper, 1944.

Brooks, Phillips. *Yale Lecture on Preaching.* New York: Dutton, 1879.

Brown, Jeff. *A Handbook for the Preacher at Work.* Grand Rapids: Baker, 1958.

Burrell, David James. *The Sermon: Its Construction and Delivery.* New York: Revell, 1913.

Caldwell, Frank. *Preaching Angles.* Nashville: Abingdon, 1954.

Clarke, James W. *Dynamic Preaching.* Westwood, N.J.: Revell, 1960.

Coffin, Henry Sloane. *Communion Through Preaching.* New York: Scribner, 1952.

Cox, Harvey. *The Secular City.* New York: Macmillan, 1966.

Dabney, Robert Lewis. *Sacred Rhetoric: Lectures on Preaching.* New York: Randolph, 1870.

Dale, R. W. *Nine Lectures on Preaching.* New York: A. S. Barns, 1877.

Davis, Ozora. *Evangelistic Preaching.* New York: Revell, 1921.

Dean, Horace F. *Operation Evangelism.* Grand Rapids: Zondervan, 1957.

Dover, John. "The Training of the First Preachers." *Preacher's Quarterly* 14 (Sept. 1968) :163.

Etter, John W. *The Preacher and His Sermon.* Dayton, Ohio: United Brethren, 1883.

Farmer, Herbert H. *The Servant of the World.* New York: Scribner, 1942.

Fisher, Wallace E. *Preaching anl Parish Renewal.* Nashville: Abingdon, 1966.

Fosdick, Harry Emerson. "What Is The Matter with Preaching?" *Harper's Magazine* 157:137.

Fritz, John Henry Charles. *Essentials of Preaching: A Refresher Course in Homiletics for Pastors.* St. Louis: Concordia, 1948.

Garrison, Webb B. *The Preacher and His Audience.* Westwood, N.J.: Revell, 1954.

Garvie, Alfred Ernest. *The Christian Preacher.* New York: Scribner, 1921.

Gilkey, Langdon. *How the Church Can Minister to the World Without Losing Itself.* New York: Harper & Row, 1964.

Gilman, Wilbur E.; Aly, Bower; and Reid, Loren D. *The Fundamentals of Speaking.* New York: Macmillan, 1951.

Graves, Henry C. *Lectures on Homiletics.* Philadelphia: Amer. Bapt., 1906.

Haselden, Kyle. *The Urgency of Preaching.* New York: Harper & Row, 1963.

Hervey, George Winfred. *Christian Rhetoric.* New York: Harper, 1873.

Hoppin, James M. *Homiletics.* New York: Mean, 1881.

Howe, Reuel L. *The Miracle of Dialogue.* New York: Seabury, 1963.

––––––. *Partners in Preaching.* New York: Seabury, 1967.

Hoyt, Arthur S. *The Preacher: His Person, Message, and Method.* New York: Macmillan, 1909.

Johnson, Herrick. *The Ideal Ministry.* New York: Revell, 1913.

Jones, Ilion Tingal. *Principles and Practice of Preaching.* New York: Abingdon, 1956.

Jordan, Gerald Ray. *You Can Preach.* New York: Revell, 1951.

Jowett, John H. *The Preacher: His Life and Work.* New York: Harper, 1912.

Jud, Gerald J. *Crisis in the Church.* Philadelphia: Pilgrim, 1968.

Kelman, John. *The War and Preaching.* London: Hodder & Stoughton, 1919.

Kern, John Adam. *The Ministry to the Congregation.* New York: Jennings & Graham, 1897.

Kidder, Daniel P. *A Treatise on Homiletics.* New York: Carlton & Lanahan, 1866.

Koller, Charles W. *Expository Preaching Without Notes.* Grand Rapids: Baker, 1962.

—————. *Sermons Preached Without Notes.* Grand Rapids: Baker, 1964.

Korzybski, Alfred. *Science and Sanity.* Lakeville, Conn.: Internat. Non-Aristotelian Library, 1948.

Lee, Irving J. *Language Habits in Human Affairs.* New York: Harper, 1941.

Lewis, Ralph L. *Speech for Persuasive Preaching.* Berne, Ind.: Economy, 1968.

MacGregor, W. M. *The Making of a Preacher.* Philadelphia: Westminster, 1946.

Maclaren, Ian. *The Cure of Souls.* New York: Dodd, Mead, 1896.

MacPherson, Ian. *The Art of Illustrating Sermons.* New York: Abingdon, 1964.

—————. *The Burden of the Lord.* New York: Abingdon, 1955.

McBurney, James H., and Hance, Kenneth G. *Discussion in Human Affairs.* New York: Harper, 1950.

McCracken, Robert J. *The Making of the Sermon.* New York: Harper, 1956.

McNeil, Jesse Jai. *The Preacher-Prophet in Mass Society.* Grand Rapids: Eerdmans, 1961.

Menzies, Robert. *Preaching and Pastoral Evangelism.* Edinburg: St. Andrew, n.d.

Meyer, F. B. *Expository Preaching: Plans and Methods.* New York: Doran, 1912.

Miller, Donald G. *The Way to Biblical Preaching*. Nashville: Abingdon, 1957.

Morgan, G. Campbell. *Preaching*. New York: Revell, 1937.

Mott, John R., ed. *Evangelism for the World Today*. New York: Harper, 1938.

Oliver, Robert T. *Psychology of Persuasive Speech*. New York: Longmans, Green, 1948.

Pattison, Thomas Harwood. *The Making of the Sermon*. Philadelphia: Amer. Bapt., 1898.

Perry, Lloyd M. *Biblical Sermon Guide*. Grand Rapids: Baker, 1970.

––––––. "Trends and Emphases in the Philosophy, Materials, and Methodology of American Protestant Homiletical Education as Established by a Study of Selected Trade and Textbooks Published between 1834 and 1954." Ph.D. diss., Northwestern U., 1961.

Perry, Lloyd M., and Culver, Robert D. *How to Search the Scriptures*. Grand Rapids: Baker, 1967.

Phelps, Arthur Stevens. *Speaking in Public*. New York: Richard R. Smith, 1930.

Phelps, Austin. *The Theory of Preaching*. London: Dickenson, 1882.

Porter, Ebenezer. *Lectures on Homiletics and Preaching, and on Public Prayer*. Andover, N.Y.: Flagg, Gould & Newman, 1834.

Price, J. M.; Chapman, J. H.; and Carpenter, L. L. *Introduction to Religious Education*. New York: Macmillan, 1932.

Randolph, David James. *The Renewal of Preaching*. Philadelphia: Fortress, 1969.

Rees, Paul S. "Five Key Elements of Effective Sermons." In *How to Prepare and Deliver Better Sermons*. Washington, D.C.: Christianity Today, n.d.

Reid, Clyde. *The Empty Pulpit*. New York: Harper & Row, 1967.

Reu, M. *Homiletics*. Chicago: Wartburg, 1922.

Richardson, Alan. *Christian Apologetics*. New York: Harper, 1947.

Roach, Corwin C. *Preaching Values in the Bible*. Louisville: Cloister, 1946.

Rockey, Carol J. *Scriptural Evangelism*. Philadelphia: Lutheran Publ., 1925.

Sanford, Jack D. *Make Your Preaching Relevant*. Nashville: Broadman, 1963.

Sarett, Lew, and Foster, W. T. *Basic Principles of Speech*. Boston: Houghton Mifflin, 1946.

Schenck, Ferdinand Schureman. *Modern Practical Theology: A Manual of Homiletics, Liturgics, Poimenics, Archagics, Pedagogy, Sociology, and the English Bible*. New York: Funk & Wagnalls, 1903.

Shedd, William G. T. *Homiletics and Pastoral Theology.* New York: Scribner, Armstrong, 1873.

Skinner, Thomas Harvey. *Aids to Revealing and Hearing.* New York: Taylor, 1893.

Sleeth, Ronald E. *Proclaiming the Word.* Nashville: Abingdon, 1964.

Smith, Charles. *Biblical Authority for Modern Preaching.* Philadelphia: Westminster, 1960.

Spurgeon, Charles H. *Great Pulpit Masters.* Vol. 2. New York: Revell, 1950.

Stanfield, V. L. *Effective Evangelistic Preaching.* Grand Rapids: Baker, 1965.

Stewart, James S. *Heralds of God.* London: Hodder & Stoughton, 1946.

Sturtevant, S. T. *The Preacher's Manual.* New York: Riker, 1840.

Sweazey, George Edgar. *Effective Evangelism.* New York: Harper, 1953.

Teikmanis, Arthur L. *Preaching and Pastoral Care.* Englewood Cliffs, N.J.: Prentice-Hall, 1964.

Thielicke, Helmut. *The Trouble with the Church.* Trans. and ed. John W. Doberstein. New York: Harper & Row, 1965.

Thompson, William D. *A Listener's Guide to Preaching.* New York: Abingdon, 1966.

Thompson, W. D. and Bennett, Gordon C. *Dialogue Preaching.* Valley Forge: Judson, 1969.

Tittle, Ernest Fremont. *The Foolishness of Preaching.* New York: Henry Holt, 1930.

Tizard, J. Leslie. *Preaching: the Art of Communication.* London: Oxford, 1958.

Truett, George W. *The Inspiration of Ideals.* Grand Rapids: Eerdmans, 1950.

Turnbull, Ralph G., ed. *Baker's Dictionary of Practical Theology.* Grand Rapids: Baker, 1967.

von Allmen, Jean Jacques. *Preaching and Congregation.* Richmond: John Knox, 1962.

Webber, F. R. *A History of Preaching in Britain and America.* 3 Vols. Milwaukee: Northwestern, 1952-57.

Whitesell, Faris D. *The Art of Biblical Preaching.* Grand Rapids: Zondervan, 1950.

————. *Power in Expository Preaching.* Westwood, N.J.: Revell, 1963.

————. *Sixty-Five Ways to Give an Evangelistic Invitation.* Grand Rapids: Zondervan, 1945.

Work, Edgar Whitaker. *Every Minister His Own Evangelist.* New York: Revell, 1927.

# Index